Garden Structures You Can Make

▪ Garden Structures You Can Make ▪

Paul Gerhards

STACKPOLE
BOOKS

Published by
STACKPOLE BOOKS
5067 Ritter Road
Mechanicsburg, PA 17055

Printed in the United States of America

Cover design by Kathleen D. Peters
Cover photograph by Paul Gerhards

First Edition

10 9 8 7 6 5 4 3 2 1

Library of Congress Cataloging-in-Publication Data

Gerhards, Paul.
    Garden structures you can make / Paul Gerhards. — 1st ed.
      p.   cm.
    ISBN 0-8117-2475-1
    1. Garden structures—Design and construction—Amateurs' manuals. I. Title.
  TH4961.G47   1996
    684. 1'8—dc20   95-46755
                                           CIP

To my father, Peter Gerhards,
who taught me the value of careful workmanship;
and to my wife, Nanci Hamilton Gerhards,
whose love for gardening was the inspiration
for many of the projects in this book

▪ Contents ▪

THE PROJECTS

▪ Introduction ▪

An estimated sixty-one million individuals across the country take pleasure in turning soil, planting seeds and bulbs, and harvesting fruits, vegetables, and flowers from backyard gardens. We prune and clip and cultivate not only for the beauty of a well-tended yard and garden, but also for the joy it brings from the doing. All this industry makes gardening the number one hobby in America.

Others among us, even though we might lack a green thumb, still take delight in a pleasant environment outside the house proper. This is especially true when we can build many of the structures and furnishings ourselves.

Presented here are fifteen do-it-yourself projects designed for the home garden or backyard patio. The projects range in difficulty and scope. Some of them, such as the window-box plant stand, can be built in one or two days; others, like the greenhouse, will take much longer.

Some knowledge of woodworking and skill with shop and hand tools is assumed, but most of the projects can easily be tackled by the novice woodworker.

And as with all woodworking projects, taking every safety precaution should be the rule. Always wear eye protection when using power tools. Never make any cut until you are sure where your fingers are in relation to the blade and its travel. Always make sure the stock is held firmly and will not be grabbed and flung out of place by the machinery.

A little bit of forethought and caution will help ensure that you'll enjoy the results of your efforts rather than recuperating after a trip to the hospital.

▪ Materials ▪

Materials you will use to build any of the projects in this book are a matter of personal choice, local availability, and of course, the project itself. You should have some knowledge of different kinds of lumber, however.

LUMBER

Softwoods suitable for outdoor construction projects are California redwood, western red cedar, Douglas fir, and in some cases, pine.

Redwood and cedar, especially the clear heartwood closest to the center of the tree, are naturally resistant to rot and decay and will last many times longer than other softwoods. Applying some sort of sealer or stain will enhance the beauty of any softwood and prolong its usefulness. Left untreated, redwood will turn nearly black with age, and cedar gray. Whereas redwood and cedar will last a long time regardless of treatment, fir and pine will give much better service if stained or painted. Neither fir nor pine should be used where the wood will be in close and continuous contact with the ground. The exception is pressure-treated wood (discussed below).

Softwoods are dimensioned and referred to by nominal rather than actual size. A board referred to as a 2×4, for example, is actually 1½×3½ inches, and 1×4 is actually ¾×3½ inches. This is a traditional reference, as the rough-cut lumber came from the mill in true nominal dimensions, and further planing reduced it to the actual dimensions.

Unless otherwise specified, all the lumber for the projects will be referred to as softwoods.

You might, however, wish to build some of the projects out of hardwood. Hardwoods are generally not available at lumberyards and home-improvement centers but through hardwood dealers. Some typical hardwoods for outdoor use are white oak, mahogany, Philippine mahogany, and teak. Check with your local dealer for availability.

Softwoods readily available are S4S—that is, surfaced, or smooth, on four sides. Hardwoods also can be purchased S4S but are more expensive than S2S, which has smooth broad sides but rough edges. As a rule, softwood lumber is ready for use as is; hardwoods will likely need further machining in the shop.

The same dimensional rule that applies to softwoods applies to hardwoods, but with a few distinctions. One-by hardwood is actually ¾ inch thick (although some mills might make it a little thicker for further machining in the shop) but is generally referred to as ¼ (four-quarter) stock. A board 1 inch thick, then, is referred to as ⁵⁄₄ (five-quarter), and so on. Also, hardwood is nearly always sold by the board foot (cubic foot), whereas softwood is retailed by the linear foot.

Treated Lumber

Treated lumber, also called pressure-treated lumber, is widely available for home use. Pressure-treated wood will last up to forty times longer than its untreated counterpart because of its extraordinary resistance to disease and decay. It is ideal for use where wood comes in direct contact with the ground. Treated lumber is usually fir or pine.

There are three categories of wood treatments used today: creosote, oil-borne preservatives (pentachlorophenal and copper naphthenate), and waterborne preservatives. The first two are used primarily in commercial and industrial applications. Lumber treated with waterborne preservatives is what you will find in lumberyards and home-improvement centers, and further mention of treated lumber will refer to this method of treatment only.

The chemicals used to treat lumber are chromated copper arsenate (CCA), ammoniacal copper zinc arsenate (ACZA), and ammoniacal copper arsenate (ACA). The common ingredient in all of these chemicals, and the one that does the most work in fighting disease and decay, is inorganic arsenic.

During the treatment process, the wood is first dried to make room for the chemicals, which are then injected into the wood or forced into the wood cells under pressure.

All chemicals used in wood preserving are regulated by the Environmental Protection Agency, but not so the treated products. Certain precautions apply:
- Always cut and machine treated wood outside.
- Wear a face mask while cutting and machining treated wood.
- Wash hands thoroughly before eating or smoking.
- Wash work clothing separately after working with treated wood.
- Dispose of sawdust and scraps as you would your household garbage. Do not burn scraps or use sawdust as a soil amendment (such as add it to your compost pile).

A complete list of precautions should be available in the form of a consumer information sheet at the point of purchase of pressure-treated lumber.

For more information on pressure-treated lumber, contact the American Wood Preservers Institute, 1945 Old Gallows Rd., Suite 550, Vienna, VA 22182, telephone (703) 893-4005, fax (703) 893-8492.

Although the AWPI declares the use of treated wood perfectly safe for applications such as raised vegetable garden beds and playground equipment, not everyone agrees. Several articles have appeared in magazines such as *Organic Gardening* (Rodale Press, 33 E. Minor, Emmaus, PA 18098, telephone (610) 967-5171) debunking studies on which the AWPI bases many of its claims.

On the use of treated lumber I make no recommendation, leaving it up to personal discretion.

HARDWARE

The bulk of the hardware used for projects in this book consists of screws ranging in lengths from 1¼ to 3 inches. In some instances, however, nails are recommended. All fastening devices and other hardware should be galvanized or plated to resist corrosion.

All references to screws are for those with trumpet heads, sometimes referred to as deck screws (the outdoor cousins of drywall screws). This kind of screw drives easily with power drivers and in most instances without first drilling pilot holes.

Some of the projects call for machine

bolts and carriage bolts. Machine bolts have hex heads and require a washer beneath the head and between the hex nut and stock. For ease of insertion, holes for machine bolts can be slightly (no more than $1/16$ inch) larger than the shank of the bolt. Carriage bolts, however, have a pan head with a squared portion beneath it. The squared portion, which is larger than the shank, is designed to grip the wood. Therefore, holes for carriage bolts *must* be of the same diameter as the shank. Otherwise you will not be able to tighten the nut sufficiently.

Hardware specific to individual projects will be discussed separately.

FINISHES

How you finish a project, as well as the degree to which a project is considered finished, is up to personal tastes. Woods like redwood and cedar, although naturally resistant to disease and decay, will retain their beauty longer if finished in some way. This is especially important for the seating and table projects, where splinters present a danger.

Finishing materials range from clear water repellents with mildewcide (not recommended for the seating or table projects), to transparent and semitransparent stains, to semigloss enamel, to spar varnish. Regardless of your choice, use the best quality you can afford and follow the manufacturer's recommendations.

One thing to consider when planning a project is the degree of finish. Is sanding necessary? Will the project be painted or stained? Will screws be set flush and left to show or counter-bored and filled? If you wish to hide obvious screws, you can first counter-bore the holes, then fill them with dowel stock or plugs. Or, if you plan to paint the project, you can fill the holes with putty or other exterior-grade filling material.

The overall appearance of many of the projects can be enhanced by using a $1/4$-inch rounding-over bit or other decorative router bit. Sometimes routing can be done after the project is finished, but other times it's best to make routed cuts before certain pieces are cut and assembled. Careful study of the plans and instructions before beginning will be your best guide on when to make decorative cuts.

▪ Project 1 ▪

WINDOW-BOX PLANT STAND

Project I Materials List

Description	Quantity	Length in feet	Comments
2×4	2	6	Legs
1" dowel	7	4	Rails
1×12	1	6	Shelving
¼" dowel			As needed for pins

The window-box plant stand is suitable for indoor or outdoor use and is easily constructed out of 2×4s for the legs, 1-inch dowels for the rails, and 1×12s for the shelves. The unit is held together with ¼-inch dowel pins.

PREPARING THE MATERIALS

To begin, select clear, straight, dry 2×4 stock for the legs. Cut each leg 36 inches long. Lay out and bore the 1-inch-diameter holes for the rails according to the dimensions shown in Figures 1.1 and 1.2. The holes for the short dowels that will form the ends of the stand go all the way through the leg stock. Make the holes that will form the sides 1¹⁄₁₆ inches deep. All the holes are centered on the inside and outside faces of the leg stock.

For best results, use a 1-inch Forstner bit for clean holes, and use a backup block to prevent the wood from splintering as the bit passes through. Also use a jig to ensure that the hole patterns are the same for each leg.

Out of 1-inch dowel stock, cut eight dowels 12⅛ inches long and six pieces 31 inches long for the rails.

Also, out of ¼-inch dowel stock, cut sixteen pins 2⅜ inches long and twelve pins 1⅝ inches long.

MAKING THE STAND

Begin assembling the stand with the ends. For each end, cut a pair of spacers 9 inches long. Brush a little glue into the holes, insert four rails into one leg, and then bring the other leg into place. Now put a spacer block between each leg at the top and bottom. Hold the assembly together with a pair of bar clamps. The rails should protrude about ¹⁄₁₆ inch from the outside surface of both legs. With the leg assembly firmly clamped together, bore a ¼-inch hole through the leg and into the dowel at each joint as shown in the inset in Figure 1.3. Use a sharp, clean-cutting bit to avoid tear-out. The holes need not go all the way through the leg but should be deep enough to fully pierce the rail (2¼ inches).

Wipe a little glue onto each 2⅜-inch pin before tapping them in place.

When the end assemblies have dried, trim the pins and sand them smooth.

Before you begin assembling the ends to one another, cut four spacers 29 inches long. Now brush glue into the remaining holes in each leg assembly. Insert the side rails, and put a spacer on both sides and the top and bottom of each leg. Hold the assembly together with pipe clamps or strap clamps.

Bore ¼-inch holes through the legs and dowels at each point. These holes can go all the way through the legs. Use a stop block to prevent the bit from tearing through the wood.

Brush a little glue onto the pins as before and tap them into place, trimming them and sanding them smooth after the glue has set.

The shelves are cut from 1×12 stock, ripped 9 inches wide and cut 36 inches long. To keep the shelves from sliding off the rails, insert two pins under the shelves at each end as shown in Figure 1.3.

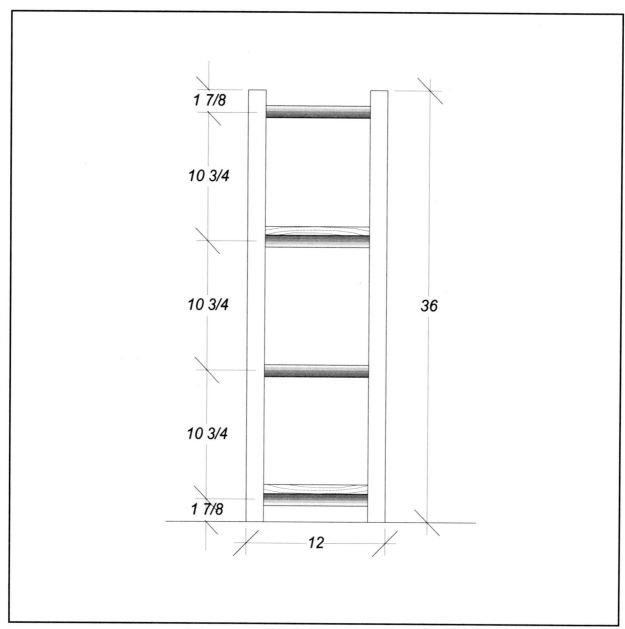

Figure 1.1. End view

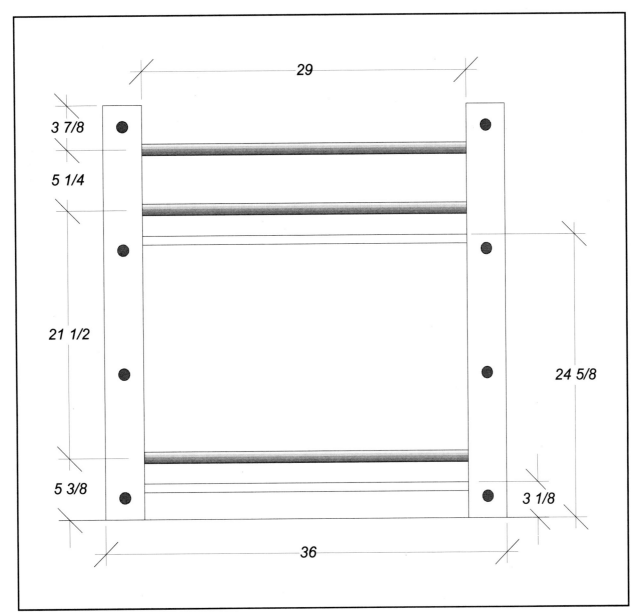

Figure 1.2. Front view

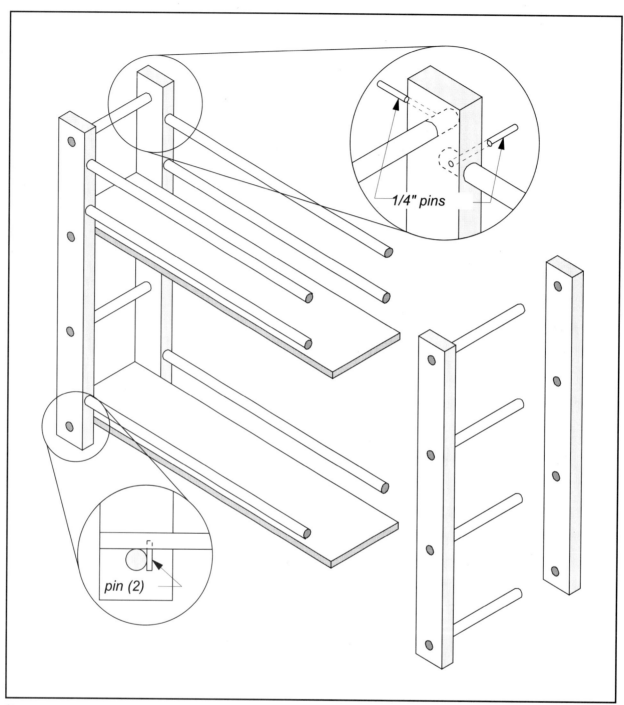

Figure 1.3. Exploded view. The upper inset shows how dowels hold the rails in place. The lower inset shows how to use pins to keep the shelves in place.

TROUGH PLANTER

The trough planter is perfect for marking a border or placing against a deck railing. It's made of ¾-inch AC plywood, 2×4s, and 1×4s. All the pieces are assembled with 1¼-inch and 1½-inch screws.

BUILDING THE BOX

The trough planter is made of two components, the box and leg assemblies. The sides and bottom of the box are cut from a single sheet of plywood. Refer to Figure 2.2 for dimensions.

Join the sides to the ends with five 1½-inch screws at each corner. Then fasten the bottom into place with a screw approximately every 12 inches.

Frame the box with rabbeted 2×4s mitered at the corners. Refer to Figure 2.1

Project 2 Materials List

Description	Quantity	Length in feet	Comments
¾" plywood	1		Sheet, AC
2×4	3	8	Box frame, legs
1×4	1	8	Collars, stretcher
1¼" screws			As needed
1½" screws			As needed

for rabbet details. Measure the pieces carefully, checking the measurements against the box before cutting. It's very easy to introduce errors when cutting miters. Tack the corners together with 6d galvanized finish nails. Mount the frame to the box with 1¼-inch screws driven through the inside about every 16 inches.

FINAL ASSEMBLY

Cut the legs out of 2×4 stock according to the dimensions shown in Figure 2.1. Lay out the legs on the box, and fasten the legs with three 1½-inch screws driven into the legs through the inside of the box. Turn the assembly upside down and attach a 1×4 collar to the inside surface of each pair of legs as shown in Figure 2.3. Use three 1½-inch screws at each joint. Measure between the collars to determine the length of the stretcher, and cut it out of a piece of 1×4. Center the stretcher and fasten it with two 1½-inch screws at each end. Upend the box and drive four or five 1½-inch screws through the bottom into the stretcher.

Drill six or eight ½-inch-diameter holes in the bottom for drainage. Apply three or four coats of good-quality latex enamel to the planter, making sure the drain holes are well sealed.

You can put dirt directly into the planter or place pots inside.

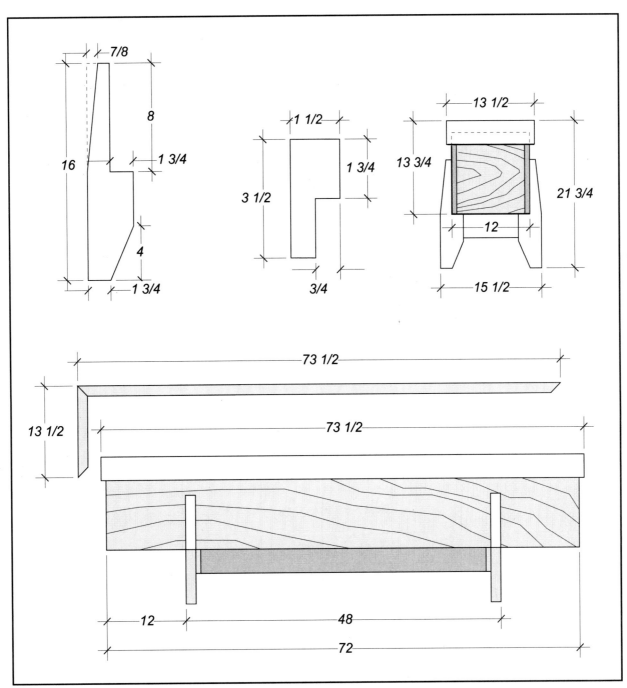

Figure 2.1. Front view, end view, leg pattern, and rail detail

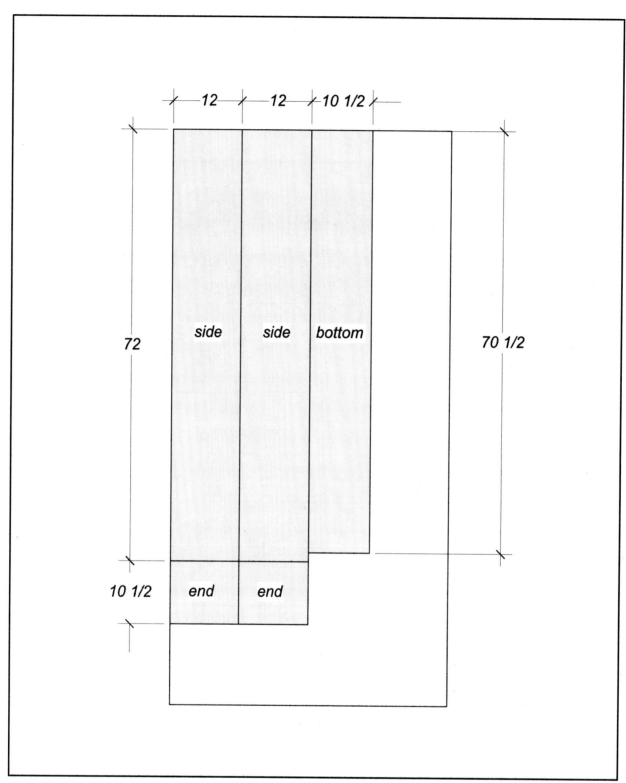

Figure 2.2. Plywood cutting patterns

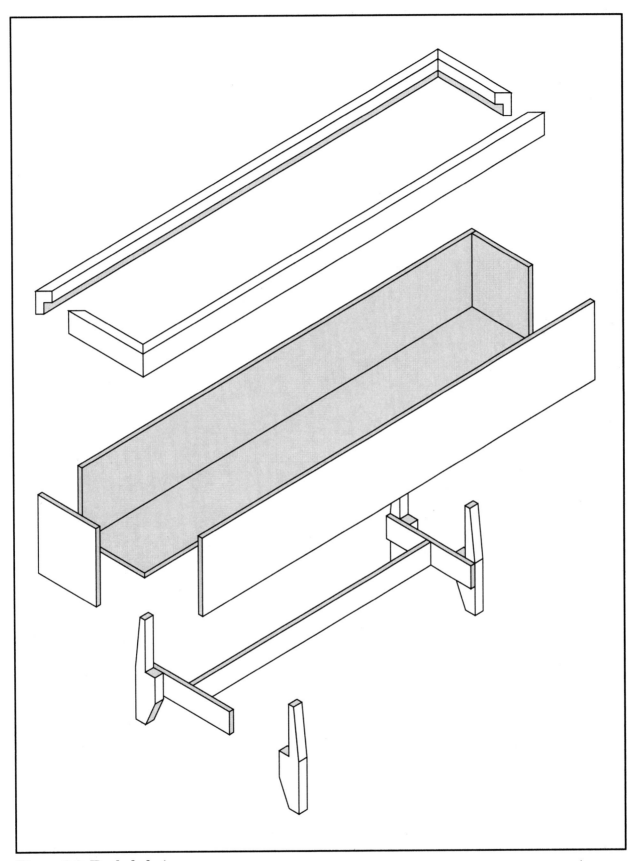

Figure 2.3. Exploded view

THREE-TIERED PLANT STAND

Project 3 Materials List

Description	Quantity	Length in feet	Comments
1×6	3	4	40½" minimum each leg
1×12		11	Shelves
Hardware, misc.			As needed

This plant stand, with its three semicircular tiers, is fairly easy to build and is suitable for interior or exterior display. Put two of them back-to-back to form a conical stand.

MAKING THE SHELVES

Refer to Figure 3.3 for the shelf geometry. Use butcher paper or craft paper to make patterns for the shelves and the legs. It's important that the notches line up exactly and the fit is snug.

Although top and middle shelves can be cut from 1×12 stock, the bottom shelf will have to be made from two or more boards joined together. The dashed lines in Figure 3.3 show how this can be done using a 1×12 and a piece at least 6 inches wide. Join the boards before making any cuts. Notice the ¼-inch dowels along the joints. These are necessary to the shelf's structural integrity.

MAKING THE LEGS

Cut the legs from 1×6 stock of at least 40½ inches long each as shown in Figure 3.4. Use butcher paper or craft paper to make the leg pattern. Lay out the pattern relative to the axis as shown.

Carefully cut out the pattern and transfer the outline to the leg stock. All three legs are the same, except the center leg requires an extra cut to keep it within the proscribed radius of the semicircular tripod. Measure

¾ inches from the axis, and make the cut perpendicular to the horizontal plane.

FINAL ASSEMBLY

Before assembling the plant stand, check that all of the slotted parts slip together easily. The fit should be snug but not so tight that it's difficult to get the pieces apart. Thoroughly sand the parts, if desired.

To begin the assembly, first join the two outside legs using ¼-inch dowels and glue as shown in the inset in Figure 3.5. To successfully clamp the pieces together while the glue sets, you will need to make a pair of clamp wedges as shown. To keep the wedges from slipping as pressure is applied, either glue a strip of sandpaper to the wedge or apply a coat or two of spray adhesive.

Next, fasten the center leg to the assembly with a pair of 1½-inch screws as shown. Be careful not to drive the screws through the dowels.

Slip the bottom and middle shelves into place. Secure them through the back side of the outer legs with screws or nails. If necessary, use a 6d nail to tack the outer legs to the shelf as shown in the lower inset in Figure 3.5. Do not, however, fasten the bottom and middle shelves to the center leg; this will allow the shelves to expand and contract freely.

Fasten the top shelf to the tripod with three 6d galvanized finish nails or 1¼-inch screws, one driven into each leg.

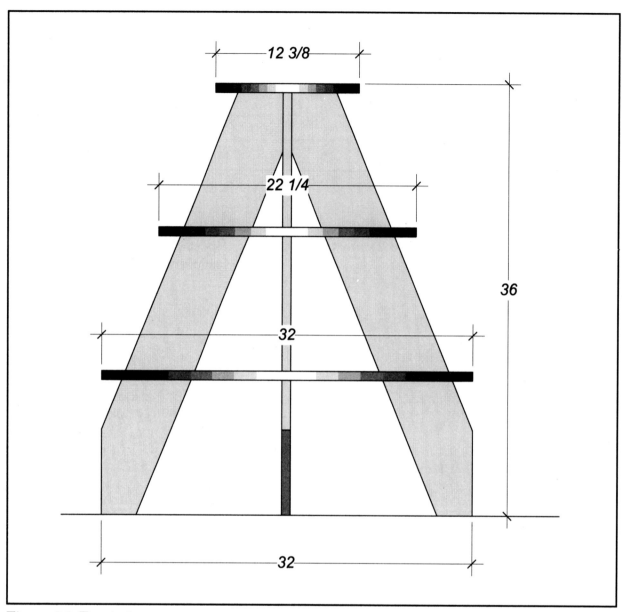

Figure 3.1. Front view

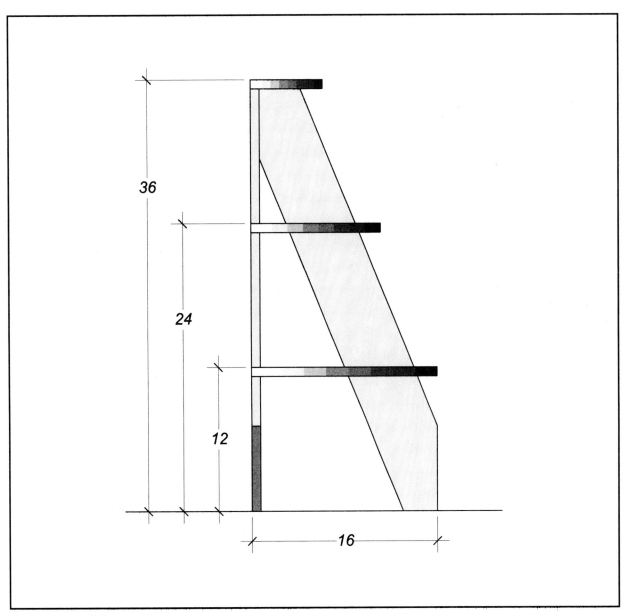

Figure 3.2. Side view

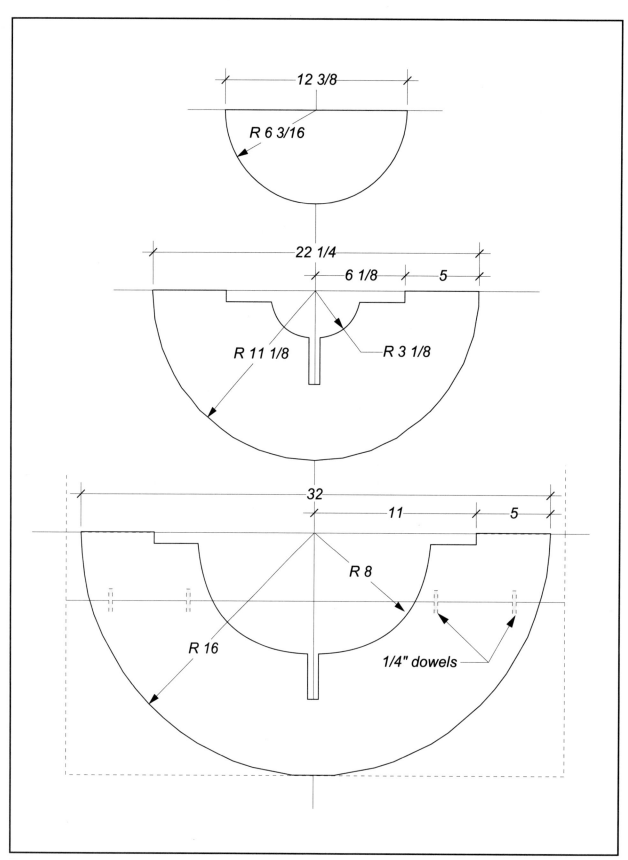

Figure 3.3. Shelf patterns

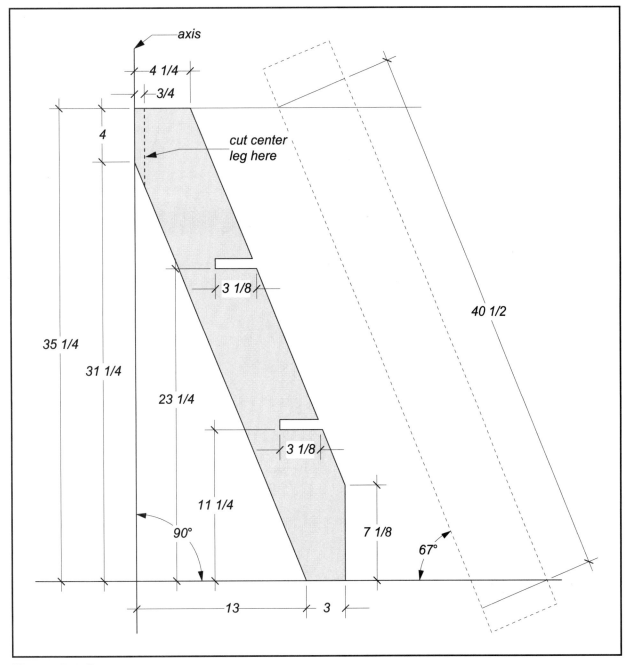

Figure 3.4. Leg pattern

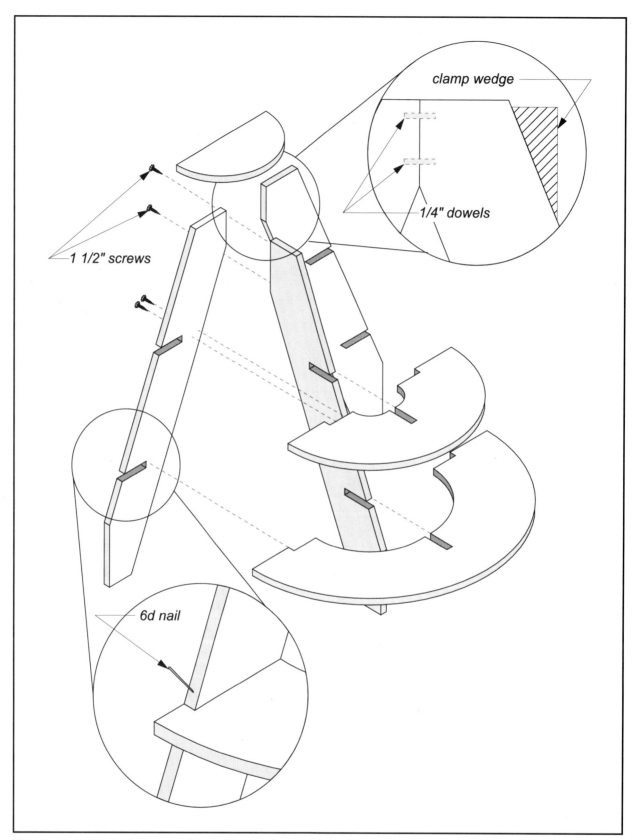

Figure 3.5. Exploded view. Upper inset shows dowel placement and the use of clamp wedges. Lower inset shows how to secure the leading edges of the outer legs to the shelves.

▪ Project 4 ▪

WISHING-WELL PLANTER

Wishing-well planters are popular lawn ornaments. You can build this one with or without a bottom, fill it with dirt, or insert a large plastic planter. The windlass and bucket are optional. You can use a galvanized bucket, or make one of wood as described here. Alternatively, you can build the well portion without the roof for use as a patio planter.

The well is made of octagonal rings composed of 2×2 segments. The model illustrated in the photograph is made according to segment lengths shown in Figure 4.3. Also included, in Figure 4.9, are dimensions for rings of four other diameters. Larger diameters are possible as well.

MAKING THE WELL

The well is made of twelve octagonal rings, each rotated 22½ degrees from the one below it. Each ring is made of eight 2×2 segments of equal length. The diameter of the ring is determined by the length of its segments. Figure 4.3 illustrates how two rings of the same diameter can be made from segments of two different lengths and angles. In the upper ring, the overall length of each segment is 10 inches, and the segments are cut at a 45-degree angle on each end. In the lower ring, the overall length of each segment is 9⅛ inches, and the ends are cut at a 22½-degree angle.

You can use either method, but the first

Project 4 Materials List

Description	Quantity	Length in feet	Comments
2×2		95	
2×4	1	8	Uprights
1×4		16	Well bottom, bucket
½" stock		28	Bender board for roof
1" dowel	1	4	
4d nails			As needed
8d nails			As needed
1¼ screws			As needed
2½" screws			As needed

one has two advantages: The wider angle presents a larger mating surface, and the pieces can be nailed together from the inside as shown in Figure 4.4.

It's important that the segments be cut accurately. They can be cut on a table saw, radial arm saw, or power miter saw with the use of a jig built specifically for the intended saw. Make certain that the stock is held firmly and *safely* in place during the cut. While making dozens of repetitive cuts, it's easy to let your mind wander; that's when fingers can be lost. Before making a cut, I always ask myself, "Where are my fingers?" and assure that they are out of harm's way.

If you choose to put a bottom in your well, cut the segments for the lowermost ring ½ inch shorter than the rest and set them aside so that they will not get mixed in with the others.

As you nail the segments together, make sure the surfaces are flush and uniform. A little practice will help you determine the right position and angle in which to drive the 4d nails so that they don't poke through the outer side.

Assemble the rings from the top down. Select the top ring and lay it upside down on the bench. Place the second ring on top of the first, and rotate it as shown in Figure 4.4. Place the third ring exactly over the first one, and so on. It's important to keep the rings in proper alignment to create a plumb and stable surface on which to fasten the uprights later. As you assemble the rings, use a framing square to ensure that each ring is exactly above the other.

For added strength, run a bead of construction adhesive between the rings before nailing them together with 8d galvanized nails.

Do not yet nail on the bottom ring. First select several 1×4s (or equivalent) for the bottom and lay them out side by side on the bench. Place the well upright on top of these boards. Then scribe a line along the inside diameter of the well. Before removing the well, number the boards and make several index marks on the boards to correspond with similar marks made along the inside of the well.

Cut the boards for the bottom along the scribed lines.

Turn the well upside down and attach the bottom ring, in the same orientation as the one preceding it. Turn the well right side up and lay in the bottom boards.

MAKING THE ROOF STRUCTURE

The roof is supported by a pair of 2×4 uprights fitted to the inside of the well and attached with at least three 2½-inch screws each. You can increase the distance between the roof and the well by making the uprights longer than specified.

Figure 4.5 illustrates all the cuts needed for assembling the roof frame. First make a pair of 30-degree cuts on the top end of each upright. Then, with your table saw or radial-arm saw set to a depth of ¾ inches, cut the recesses where the rafters will sit.

Cut four rafters out of 2×2 stock 15⅛ inches long and with parallel 30-degree angles at each end. The rafter braces are also cut from 2×2 stock. Make them 10 inches long with opposing 30-degree angles on each end. As with the uprights, cut a ¾-inch-deep recess at the lower end of each brace, as shown in the inset in Figure 4.5.

Check the fit of all the pieces to ensure that each of the completed roof frames will be the same. Tack a pair of rafters together with two 4d nails or 1¼-inch screws driven through the peak. Next, secure the rafter assembly to the upright using two 1¼-inch screws driven through the inside of the upright into the rafters.

Lay the assembly flat on the bench, inside down. Bring a pair of braces into place. Make sure they are centered on the upright and meet 11¾ inches from the peak. Fasten each to the upright with a 1¼-inch screw. Drive two screws through the bottom of each brace into the rafter to finish the rafter assembly.

If you plan to install a windlass, cut a diamond-shaped spacer as shown. Tack the spacer into place with 4d nails and construction adhesive. Drive the nails well outside the area where you will next bore a hole with a 1⅛-inch diameter for the windlass.

Place each rafter assembly into the well, and tack them into place. Before securing them in place, check that they are plumb and in line with one another.

Although you can make the roof out of plywood and asphalt shingles, an attractive alternative is ½-inch bender board as shown in Figure 4.6. (Cedar bender board comes in thicknesses of ¼ inch and ½ inch and is 3½ inches wide. It is used as a lawn edging and can bend to some degree to go around curves.) Rip a starter strip of about 1 inch and tack it in place. Next, lay out the roofing material on the rafters and space them evenly to the peak. Mark the spacing, then nail the boards into place, working your way up from the bottom. Let the roofing material extend beyond the rafters an inch or two on both sides.

MAKING THE WINDLASS AND BUCKET

Refer to Figure 4.7 for the windlass assembly details. It is made from 1-inch dowel and ¾-inch scrap.

Although you can use a small galvanized bucket to finish off your wishing well, you might choose to make a wooden bucket. Figure 4.8 shows how to make a simple 8-inch-diameter bucket. First select enough 1×4 stock to yield eight 8-inch pieces for the staves. Rip the stock 3¹⁄₁₆ inches wide with 22½-degree angles on each edge, and cut the pieces to length. Then make a ¾×⅜-inch dado about ¾ inches up from the bottom edge. Cut the octagonal bottom from 1×8 stock or plywood as shown. Use small nails to tack the staves to the bottom, then tighten a band of 10-gauge copper wire around the bottom and top of the bucket. Use nylon rope for the handle and to hang the bucket from the windlass.

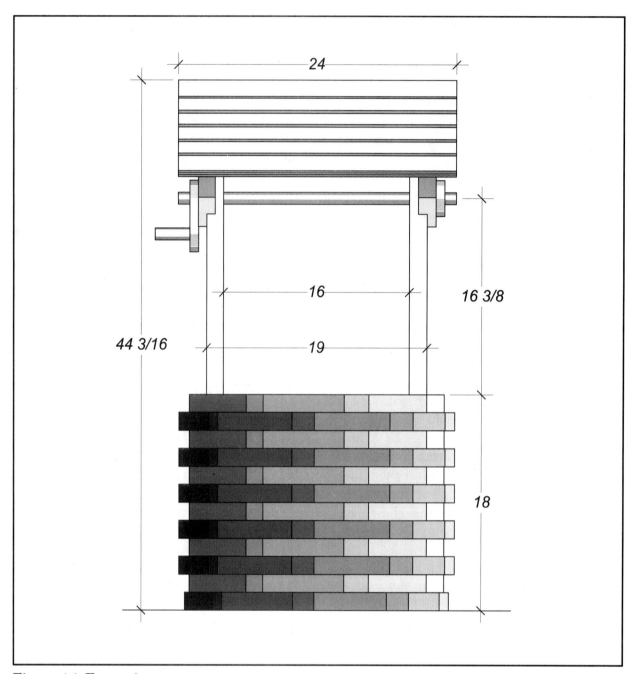

Figure 4.1. Front view

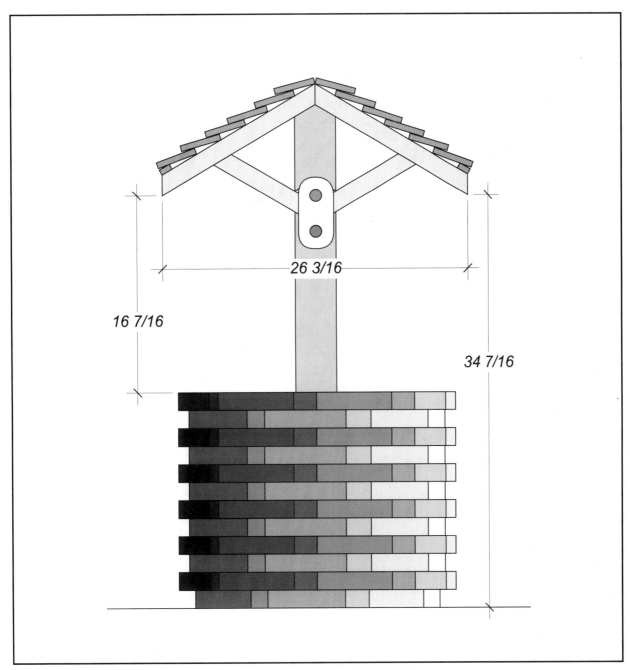

Figure 4.2. Side view

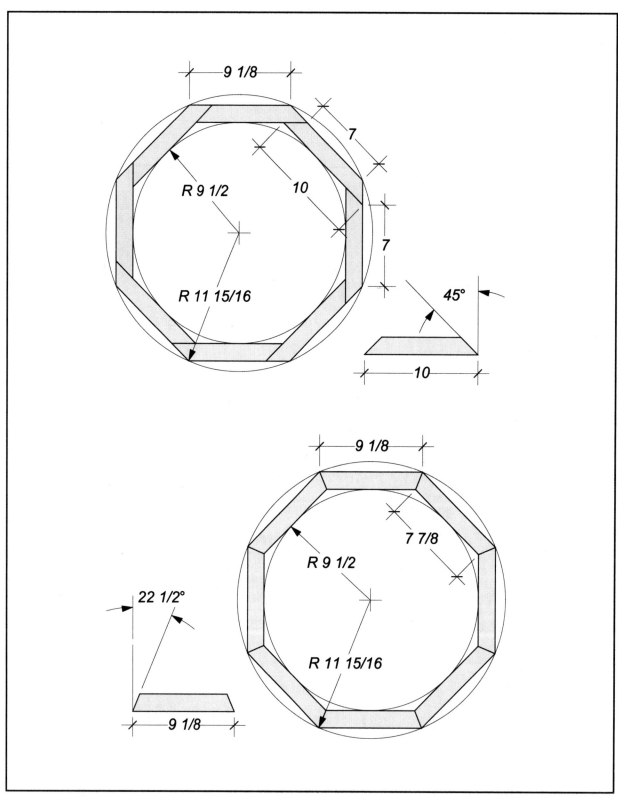

Figure 4.3. Ring detail showing two cutting variations. The upper drawing shows the segments cut at a 45-degree angle to an overall length of 10 inches. The lower drawing shows the segments cut at a 22½-degree angle to an overall length of 9⅛ inches. Both methods yield rings with the same diameter.

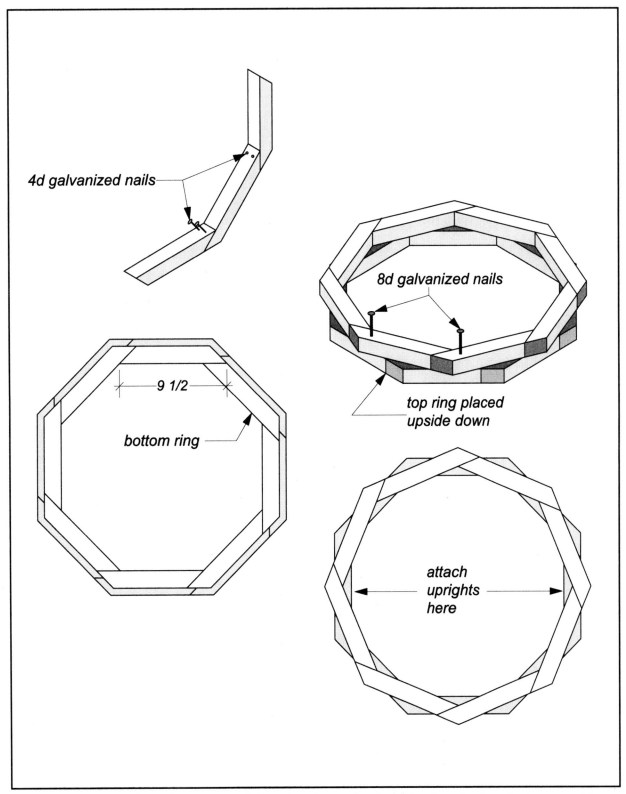

Figure 4.4. Assembling the rings and forming the well. Use 4d galvanized nails to assemble the segments into rings. Build the well upside down from the top ring down using 8d nails. The smaller bottom ring supports the well bottom. Align alternate rings carefully to ensure a uniform surface on which to mount the uprights.

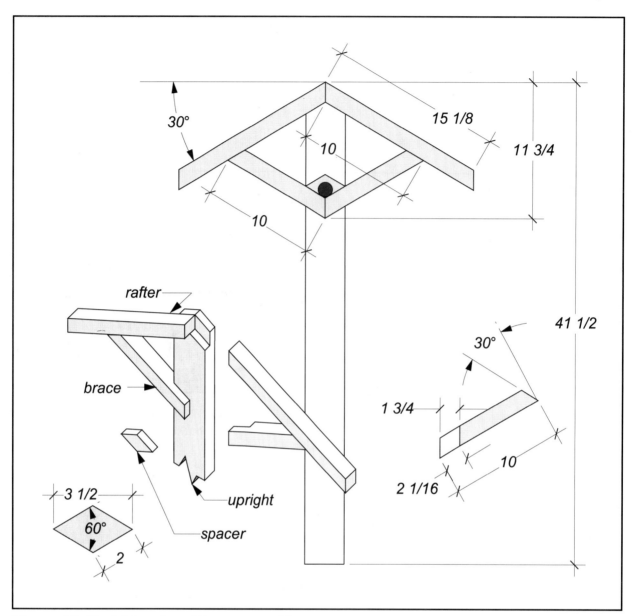

Figure 4.5. Upright and roof frame assembly

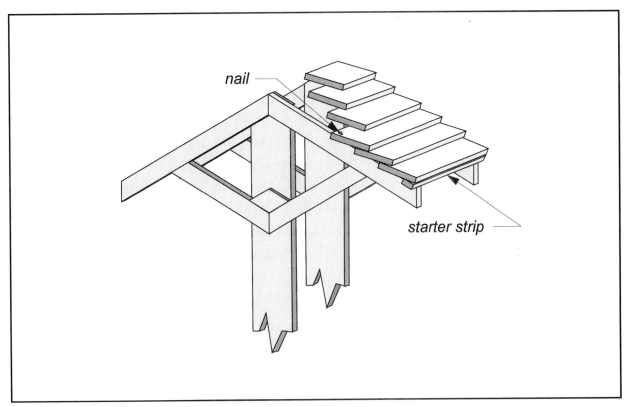

Figure 4.6. Use ¼- or ½-inch cedar bender board for roof.

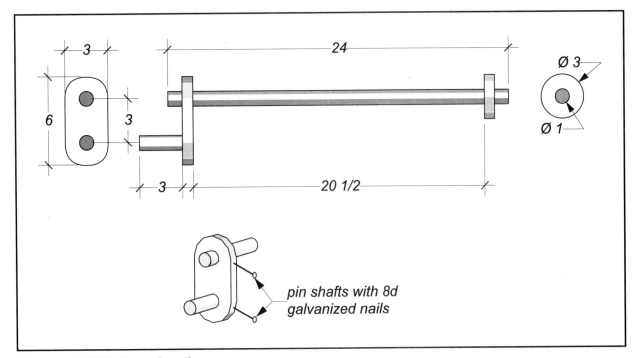

Figure 4.7. Windlass detail

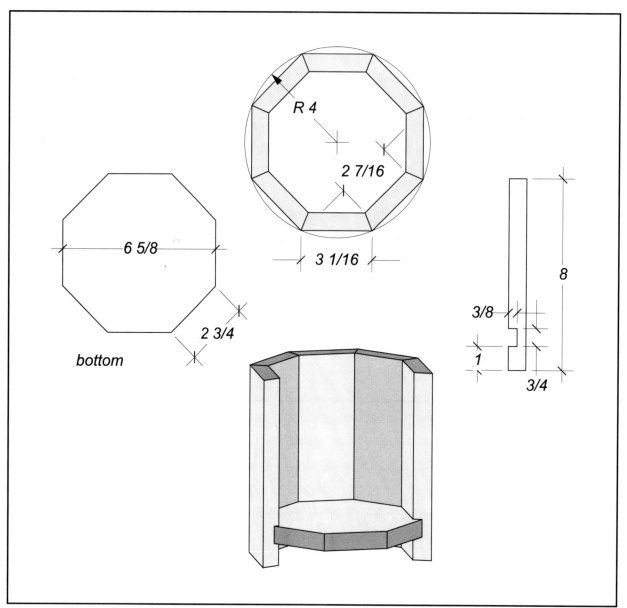

Figure 4.8. Wooden bucket detail

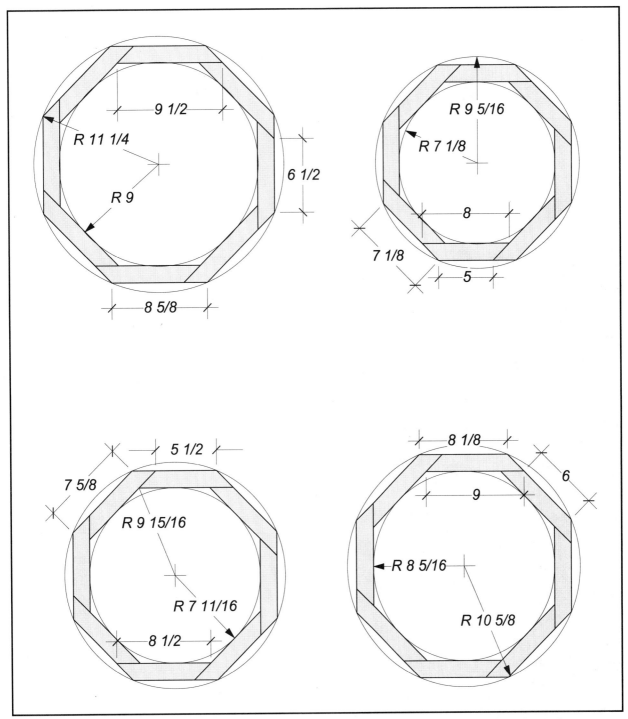

Figure 4.9. Four planter diameters derived from segment lengths of 8 inches, 8½ inches, 9 inches, and 9½ inches

PLANT TREE

A plant tree is a wonderful way to display hanging plants and bird feeders. Here's a simple design with eight stations. It's 8 feet tall and mounted to a sturdy base for portability. If you wish, you can install a longer post directly into the ground.

MAKING THE STAND

Begin the stand by making the two notched crosspieces from 2×6 stock to form the base as shown in Figures 5.2 and 5.3. Cut the notches with a jigsaw or band saw. Take care in making the notches. The pieces should fit together neatly but not so tight that it's difficult to get them apart.

A notched pedestal fits over the crosspieces. Out of 2×8 stock, rip four pieces 6½ inches wide and mitered on each edge with a 45-degree angle. Make a test cut first to ensure that the inside surface will be exactly as wide as the post. Cut each of the four pieces 16 inches long. Bevel the top edge, then cut a 1½×5½-inch notch in the center of each one as shown.

Check the fit of all the pieces before assembling the stand. Use 2½-inch screws to mount the pedestal to the base and 1½-inch screws to hold the miters together as shown in Figure 5.3. Then mount four 1×2×3-inch feet to the bottom of the stand.

FINAL ASSEMBLY

Cut a 4×4 post 90½ iches long, then lay out the notches for the crossmembers, one on

Project 5 Materials List

Description	Quantity	Length in feet	Comments
2×6		6	Base
2×8		6	Pedestal
4×4	1	8	Post
2×4	4	2'8"	Crossmembers
1×2		1	Feet
1½" screws			As needed
2½" screws			As needed

each of the four sides as shown in Figure 5.1. The uppermost crossmember is 6 inches from the top of the post. The remaining cross members are placed 11 inches on center from each other. Use a radial arm saw or a circular saw set to 1½ inches and make several passes through the layout marks to make the notches. Knock out the waste and finish the notches with a chisel.

Cut four crossmembers 31½ inches long out of 2×4 stock, and check their fit in the notches. Referring to Figure 5.1, lay out and cut the bevels on the underside of each crossmember. Finish the crossmembers by rounding the upper edges using a block plane or router. Don't, however, round the edges where they intersect the post.

Slip the post into the base and secure it with two 2½-inch screws driven through each face of the pedestal. Finally, mount the crossmembers in their notches, using two or three 2½-inch screws each.

To hang your plants and bird feeders, simply loop their hangers over the crossmembers or install heavy-gauge screw hooks where desired. Keeping larger, heavier plants near the bottom will greatly increase the tree's stability.

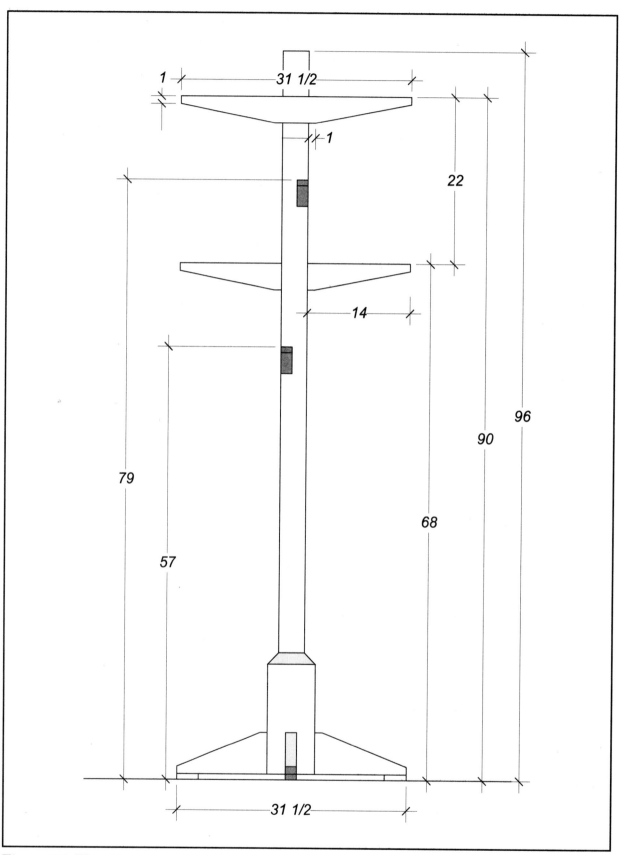

Figure 5.1. Elevation

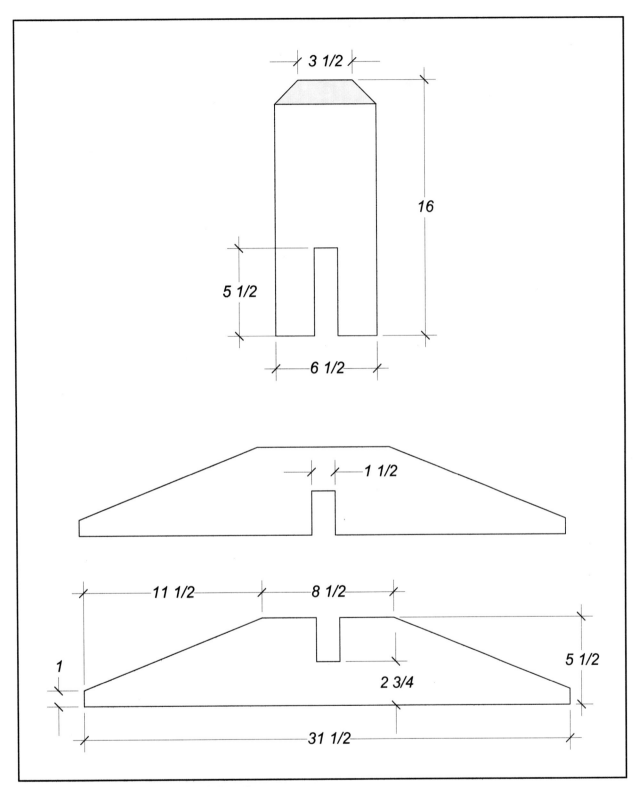

Figure 5.2. Base and pedestal detail

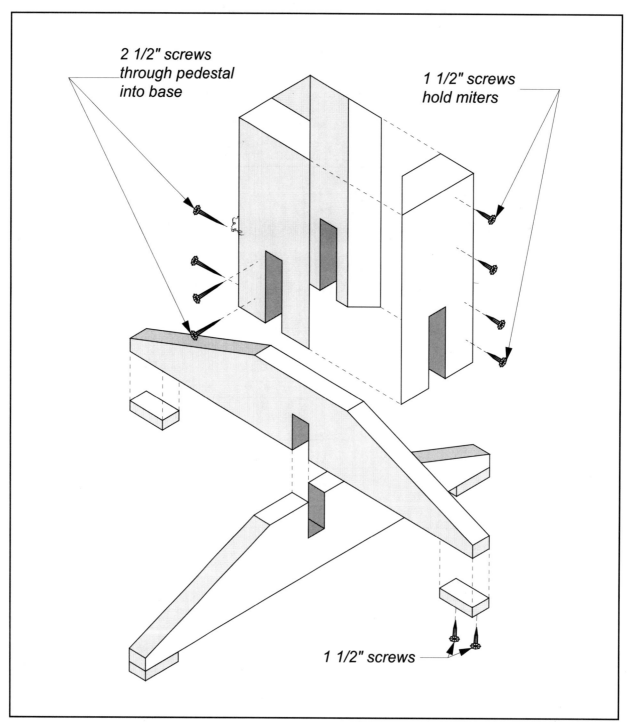

2 1/2" screws through pedestal into base

1 1/2" screws hold miters

1 1/2" screws

Figure 5.3. Exploded view of the stand

CLASSIC ONE-PIECE PICNIC TABLE

Need something in a hurry for an unexpected backyard party? You can easily build this classic picnic table out of 2×4s, 2×6s, and 2×8s in a couple of hours.

PREPARING THE PIECES
Precut all the pieces to the dimensions shown in Figures 6.1 and 6.2. Cut the legs,

braces, cleats, and top supports out of 2×4 stock. Cut the bench and bench supports out of 2×6 stock. The tabletop is made from five 2×8s (or three 2×12s). Cut the bottom corners off the top supports and seat supports as indicated.

On a large, flat surface, such as a patio or garage floor, snap two parallel lines 28½

Project 6 Materials List

Description	Quantity	Length in feet	Comments
2×8	5	5	Tabletop
2×6	6	5	Benches, bench supports
2×4	2	8	Legs, braces, top supports, cleats
Carriage bolts	16		⅜"×3½" with washers and nuts
2½" screws			As needed
3" screws			As needed
8d nails			As needed

inches apart. Place a pair of legs on the lines as shown in Figure 6.3.

Center a bench support across the legs 16½ inches above the bottom. Center a top support flush with tops of the legs. Temporarily tack the supports to the legs with 8d nails and recheck your measurements. Lay out and bore the ⅜-inch-diameter holes for the carriage bolts as indicated in Figure 6.1 (use a backing board so that you don't bore into the floor!). Separate the pieces and remove the nails. Before separating the boards, however, mark them so that the pieces won't get mixed up and each side will be assembled later as drilled.

FINAL ASSEMBLY

Begin the assembly with the top. Center a 2×8 over the top supports, letting it overhang 8½ inches on each end. Drive a 3-inch screw through the center of the 2×8 into the top support, making sure that the 2×8 and the support are square to one another. Lay the other 2×8s on the supports, spacing them about ⅛ inch apart. This will give you a top about 38 inches wide and extending beyond the supports by about 1 inch on each side. Check that the top is square by measuring the diagonals, and be certain that supports are perpendicular to the top.

Once you have everything in the right place, secure the top with two 3-inch screws at each end.

Turn the top assembly upside down. Cut a 2×4 cleat 36 inches long and center it on the underside of the top. Drive one 2½-inch screw through the cleat into each of the 2×8s.

Bolt the legs to the top supports and then the bench supports to the legs with ⅜×3½-inch carriage bolts.

Center the braces on the top and bench supports. Making sure that the leg assemblies are square with the top, tack each brace to the underside of the top with an 8d nail, then drive two 3-inch screws through the outside of the leg supports and into the ends of the brace.

Turn the table right side up, and drive two 3-inch screws through the top and into the upper end of each brace.

Using two 3-inch screws at the end of each board, mount the 2×6 bench pieces to their supports. Let the outermost boards extend 1 inch beyond the supports at the sides and 8½ inches at the ends. Space the adjacent boards about ⅛ inch apart.

Finally, cut two 10-inch cleats and fasten one onto the underside of each bench with 2½-inch screws.

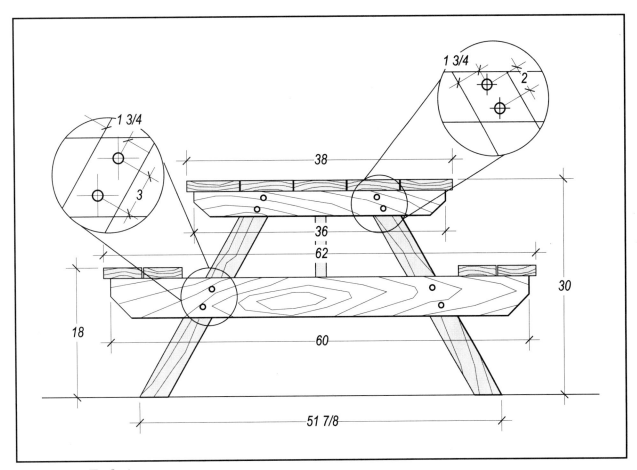

Figure 6.1. End view

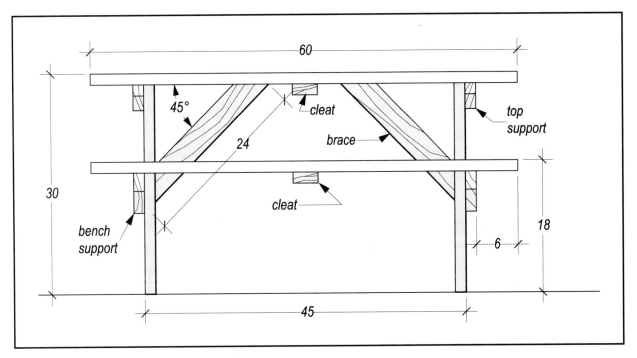

Figure 6.2. Side view

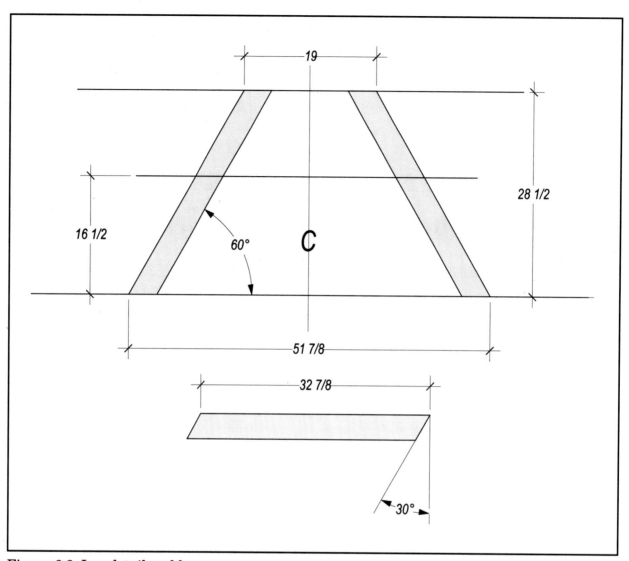

Figure 6.3. Leg detail and layout

▪ Project 7 ▪

PICNIC TABLE WITH BENCHES

Just days before I hosted a family reunion several years ago, I took a more versatile approach to making table space: I built two of these table and bench sets. The table is made of a frame of 2×4s topped with three 1×12 pine boards. The benches—two long and two short—are made of 1×12 and 1×6 pine boards. Figure 7.8 shows how to cut the 1×12s.

MAKING THE TABLE
Begin making the table by cutting two lengths of 2×4 stock 66 inches long and three 27 inches long for the frame assembly. Use 3-inch screws to assemble these pieces as shown in Figure 7.3. Use a framing square or measure the diagonals to make sure the frame assembly is square (when the diagonal measurements are the same, the frame is square).

Cut three 1×12 boards 72 inches long for the top, and place them on the table assembly. Arrange the boards so that they are evenly spaced, overhanging the ends of the frame by 3 inches and the sides by approximately 2 inches. Mount the top to

Project 7 Materials List

Description	Quantity	Length in feet	Comments
2×4	6	8	Table frame
1×12	6	8	Tabletop, benches
1×6	2	8	Stretchers
1¼" screws			As needed
2½" screws			As needed
3" screws			As needed

the frame with 1¼-inch screws—three in each board at the ends and center, and one about every 12 inches along the sides. Turn the top upside down.

Cut the legs to length with 5-degree angles on each end as shown in Figure 7.4. Also cut the notches for the end stretchers. To make the notches, make several passes through the waste area with a circular saw or radial arm saw set at 1½ inches. Knock out the waste, and finish the notch with a chisel.

Cut two stretchers 27 inches long and screw them into place with 3-inch screws. Mount the leg assemblies with 2½-inch screws as shown in the inset in Figure 7.4.

Cut the main stretcher with opposing 5-degree angles on each end. Figure 7.1 indicates a length of 59¼ inches. This dimension assumes the accuracy of the assembly so far. It might be necessary to adjust the dimension to suit your needs. Center the main stretcher relative to the end stretchers, and secure it at both ends with 3-inch screws.

MAKING THE BENCHES

Refer to Figures 7.5, 7.6, and 7.7 for bench dimensions and details. Assembly procedures are the same for both the long and short benches, and instructions are given here for a single bench.

Cut the seat to length and set it aside. Cut the legs to length with parallel 5-degree angles on each end. Lop the corners of the seat and bottom corners of the legs as shown.

To make the keyhole cutouts on the legs, place a mark along the vertical centerline 6 inches up from the bottom of each leg. Measure 3 inches in from each outer edge and place a mark along the bottom edge. Connect these marks. Measure down ½ inch from the intersection of the lines, and bore a 1-inch-diameter hole at this point. Cut along the angled lines to complete the keyhole.

The next step is to center a pair of 1×1×5-inch cleats on the inside of each leg as shown in Figure 7.6. Use a 1×6 spacer to ensure the eventual good fit of the stretcher. Apply glue to the cleats and secure them with 1¼-inch screws.

Now apply glue between the cleats and insert a 1×6 stretcher, cut to length with opposing 5-degree angles. The stretcher should be flush with the upper edge of the legs. Secure with 1¼-inch screws.

Finally, mount the seat as shown in Figure 7.7, making sure the legs are square with the seat.

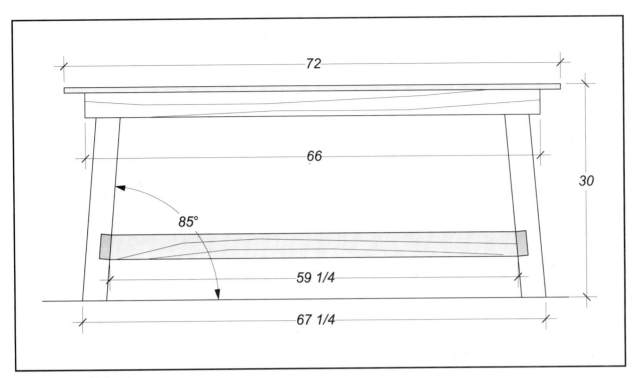

Figure 7.1. Side view

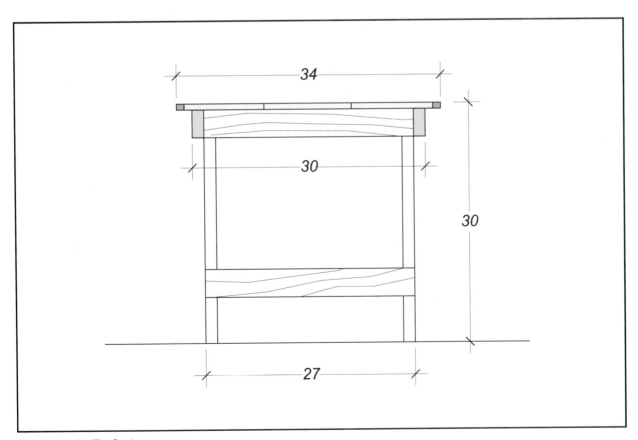

Figure 7.2. End view

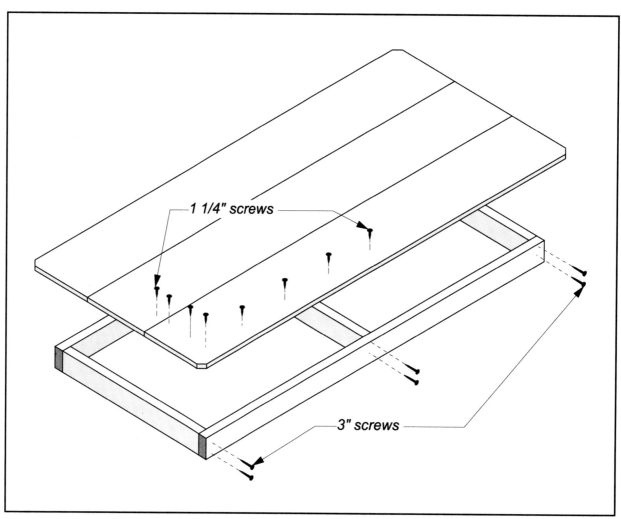

Figure 7.3. Assembling the top

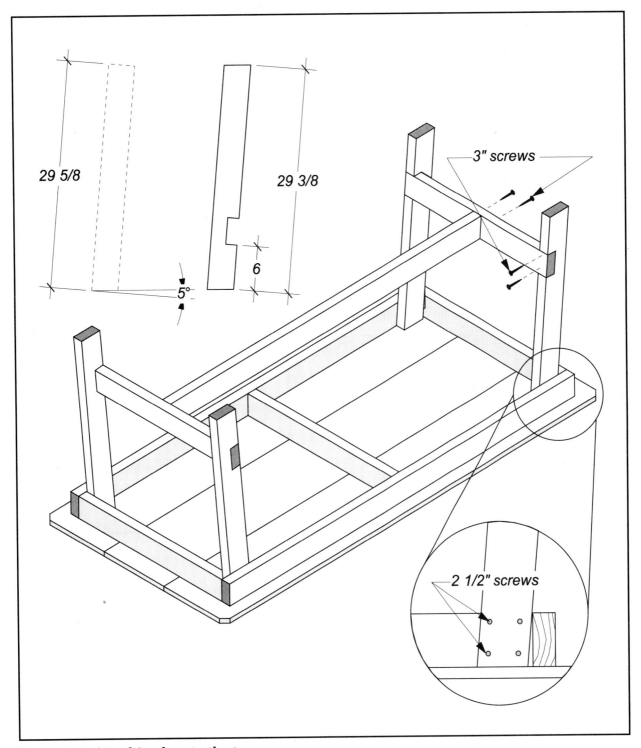

Figure 7.4. Attaching legs to the top

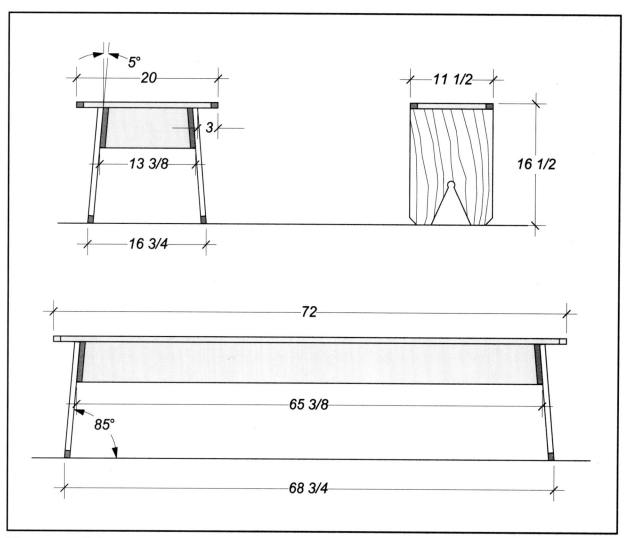

Figure 7.5. Side and end views of the benches

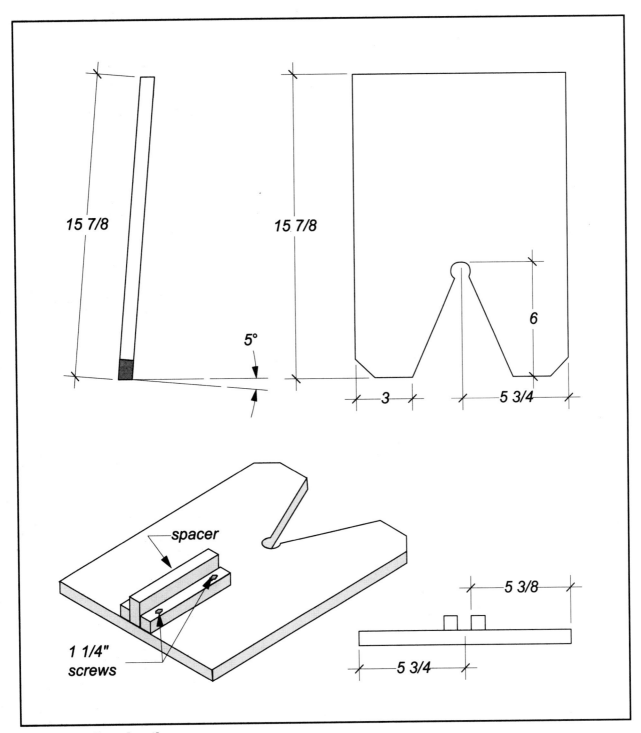

Figure 7.6. Leg detail

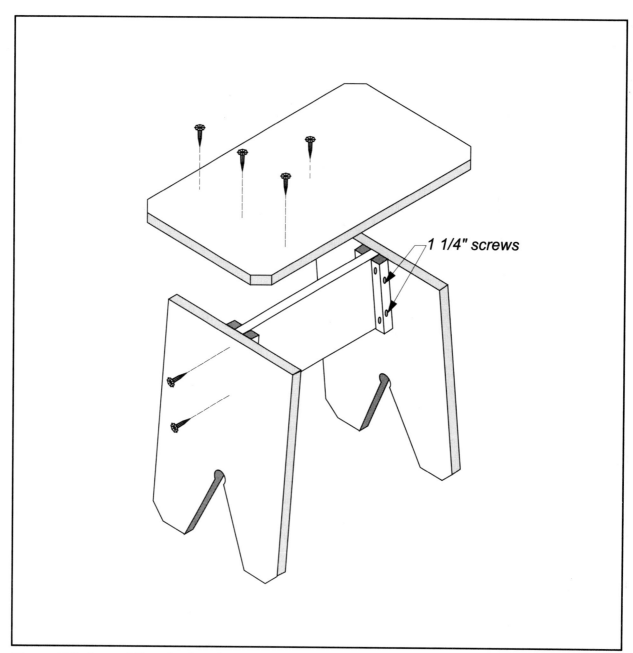

1 1/4" screws

Figure 7.7. Assembling the bench

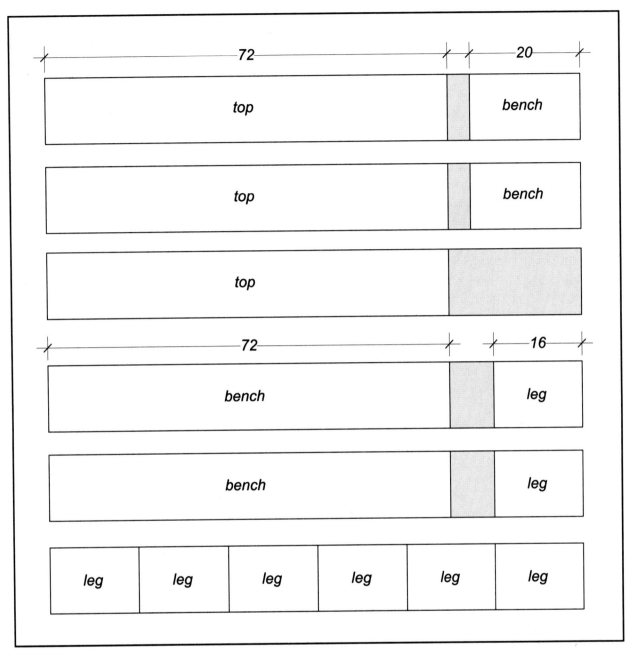

Figure 7.8. Cutting scheme

▪ Project 8 ▪

ARCHED ARBOR

There is perhaps no more inviting entry to a garden than an archway draped with roses or clematis. This arched arbor, with arches made of segments of 1×8 stock rather than cut from plywood, offers a rewarding challenge to the woodworker resulting in an eye-catching focal point of the garden.

MAKING THE ARCHES

Each of the two arches is made up of two separate sections of overlapping segments. The outer section has three segments, the inner section four. Each segment is cut from a length of 1×8, as shown in Figure 8.2. The inner section extends 6 inches below the outer section, forming half-laps to match those cut into the 2×4 uprights.

The first step is to make an accurate pattern of the arch. Use a large sheet of heavy paper, one at least 32×50 inches. (It might be necessary to tape smaller pieces together to get the right size.) Carefully study the geometry in Figures 8.1 and 8.2. When finished, your pattern will resemble the middle drawing in Figure 8.2, which includes the 6-inch tails that will form the half-lap. Notice, however, that the point from which the radius is drawn is 6 inches above the bottom of the tails. To draw the arches, use a straight stick about 30 inches long. Drive a small nail through one end of the stick to serve as a pivot. From that point, measure out 20½ inches and 24 inches toward the other end. Mark these points and bore a pencil-size hole through each. Scribe each arch. Carefully cut the pattern, being sure to leave the tails.

Cut the lengths of 1×8 to the dimensions and angles shown. With judicious planning, you can get all fourteen pieces out of four 8-foot pieces of 1×8. All of the mating angles on the outer section are 30 degrees. The two outer segments of the inner section are cut at 45 degrees, and the inner segments are cut at 30 degrees at the top and 15 degrees at the bottom.

Next, place the 1×8 segments on the bench and trace the pattern on them. Now, using a band saw or saber saw, rough-cut the arches—that is, cut about ⅜ inches outside of the line.

Once again lay the outer segments on the bench, then place the inner segments on top. Carefully check the alignment, the lap, and the diameter (48 inches across the tails). Lay your pattern on the arch as a final check.

Now, working one segment at a time, assemble the segments with construction adhesive and 1¼-inch screws as shown in Figure 8.2.

When both the arches are assembled in the rough, once again trace the pattern onto

Project 8 Materials List

Description	Quantity	Length in feet	Comments
2×4	5	8	Uprights, rails
1×8	4	8	Arches
1×2	7	2'6"	Crosspieces
¼" lattice		78	Or equivalent
1¼" screws			As needed
2½" screws			As needed
Adhesive	2		Tubes

them, and make a closer cut. Temporarily screw both arches together, and sand them smooth as a single unit.

BUILDING THE MAIN ASSEMBLY

Before proceeding with the assembly, determine what kind of lattice you will use and how you will install it. The lattice shown in the photograph is cut from lengths of ¼-inch bender board. (Cedar bender board comes in thicknesses of ¼ inch and ½ inch and is 3½ inches wide. It is used as a lawn edging and can bend to some degree to go around curves.) This lattice was assembled piece by piece into ½×½-inch dadoes routed into the uprights and rails (see Figure 8.3). Alternatively, you can buy prefabricated lattice panels, which come in widths of 12, 16, 24, and 48 inches. You can slip a panel into dadoes during assembly, or you can sandwich it between 1×1s later (see Figure 9.6). The method you choose will have a bearing on the length of the rails, and therefore the overall depth of the arbor.

Select four 2×4s to use as uprights. Cut them 72 inches long, then cut the 6-inch half-laps at the top of each, as shown in Figure 8.2. Cut four rails 24 inches long, and lay out the position of the rails on the uprights. Next, rout the dadoes in the uprights and rails. Then attach the uprights to the arches, using construction adhesive and four 1¼-inch screws at each joint as shown. Make sure the uprights are parallel. To keep them in place, fasten a temporary brace near the bottom (Figure 8.1). Make each end equidistant from the bottoms of the uprights so that you can use the brace as a leveling aid during installation.

Before installing the rails, place the two arch assemblies together and lay out the 1×2 crosspieces as shown in Figure 8.1.

Now install the rails, using two 2½-inch screws at each joint as shown. Then cut seven 1×2s 30 inches long, and fasten them over the arch with a single 1¼-inch screw at each end.

INSTALLING THE LATTICE

The arbor in the photograph has six vertical strips and nine horizontal strips of lattice on each side. The strips are 1¾ inches wide. The width, spacing, and number of strips are arbitrary—I didn't lay out the latticework, but tapped the pieces around until they looked right.

Run a thin bead of construction adhesive around the dadoes on the inside and the outside. Working quickly, fit first the vertical strips to the inside, and then the horizontal strips to the outside, making sure the strips around the perimeter are well seated in the dadoes.

Once all the strips are aligned as you like them, put a dab of adhesive between each overlap, and squeeze them together. After the adhesive has dried, pare away any excess with a sharp chisel.

FINAL INSTALLATION

To anchor your arbor in place, dig four 12-inch-deep holes. Place the arbor in the holes, and level it by tamping dirt under the uprights as needed. When the unit is level all around, fill the holes and tamp lightly. Alternatively, you can fill the holes with gravel, which will help drain water away from the wood.

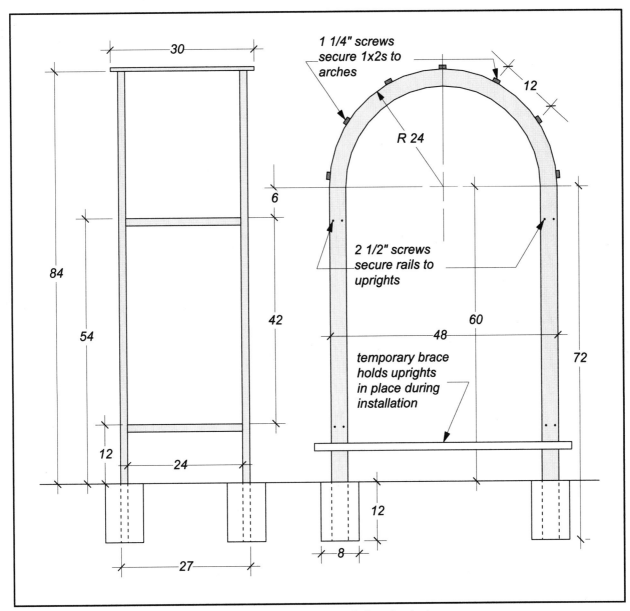

Figure 8.1. Side and front elevations (lattice removed for clarity)

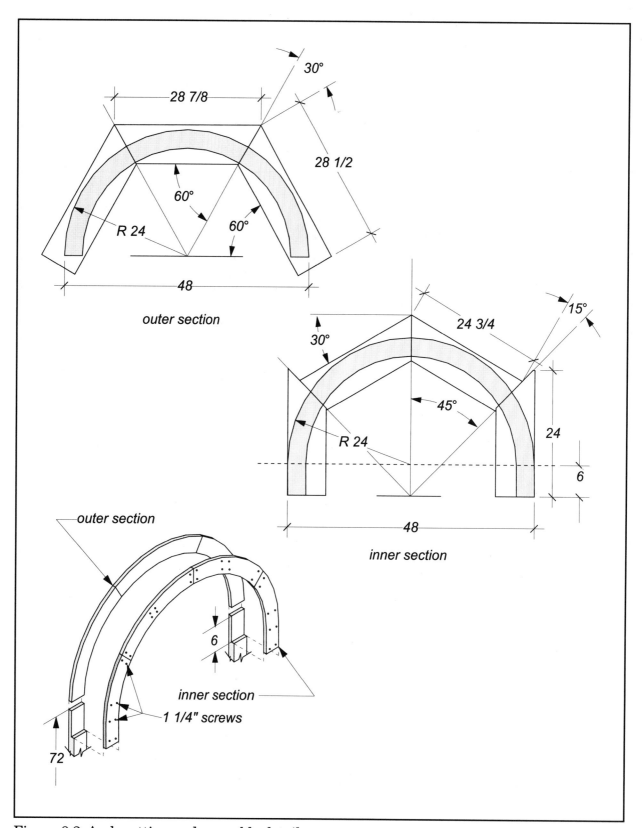

Figure 8.2. Arch cutting and assembly detail

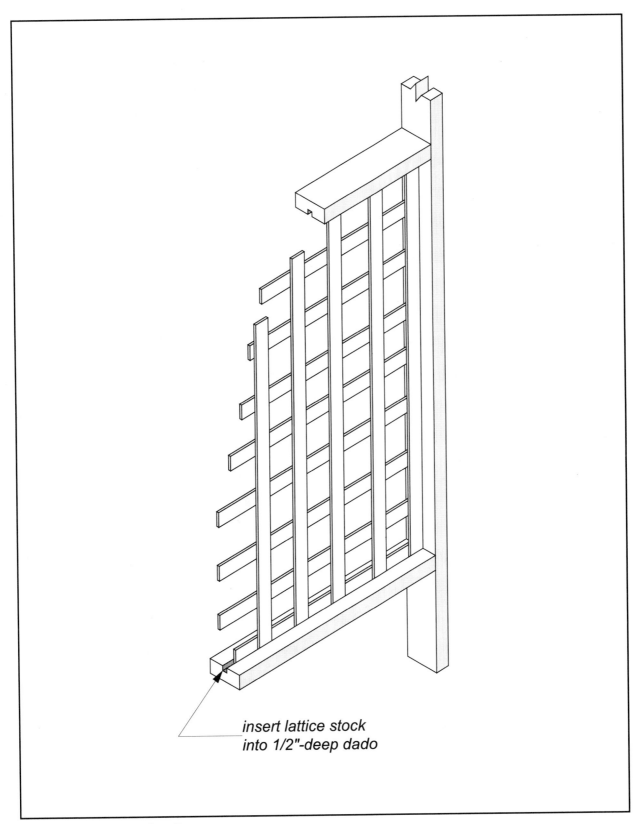

insert lattice stock
into 1/2"-deep dado

Figure 8.3. Lattice detail

▪ Project 9 ▪
INTIMATE ARBOR

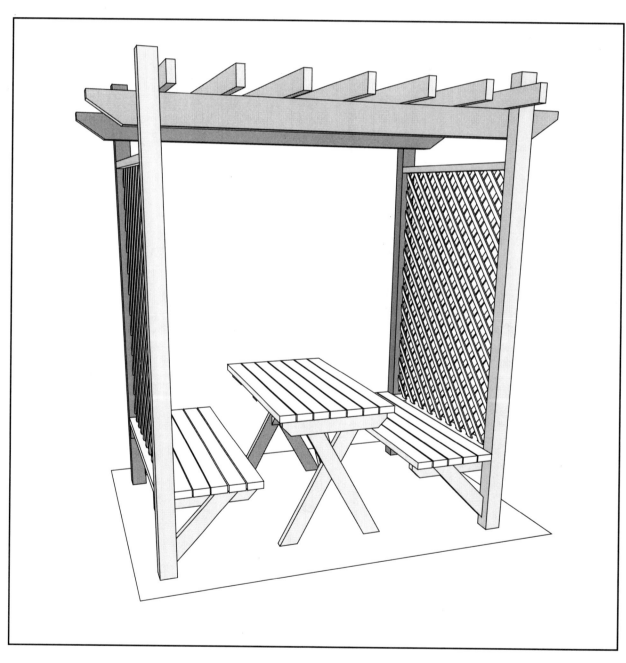

Imagine sharing a meal with someone special on a balmy summer evening within this intimate arbor. Or eliminate the table and have a classy garden gateway. This sturdy design is even suitable for a main entry.

MAKING THE ARBOR

Select a level site on which to build your arbor. It's important that the posts be square and plumb. To accurately locate the corners, you can use builders' string stretched between batter boards or, for a faster, less fussy method, use a sheet of ½-inch plywood or oriented strand board (OSB) with a pair of 2×4s fastened to it as a jig (see Figure 9.10).

Dig a hole about 12 inches in diameter and 18 inches deep, and put a couple inches of gravel in the bottom for drainage. Place the 4×4×10-foot posts in the holes and square them up. Brace them securely and recheck for square and plumb. Pour concrete, using about one sackful for each post, or for a less permanent installation, embed the posts in gravel. Allow the concrete to set firmly—at least twenty-four hours.

Then, to ensure that all relative points are level, measure one post 96 inches up from the ground, and trim the top of the post to this point. Using a level and straightedge, carefully mark the tops of the other posts and saw them off. Now you can measure down from the tops to locate the relative points.

Measure down 12 inches from the top of each post, and mount temporary ledgers at these points as shown in Figure 9.2. Use screws for easy removal.

Select your 4×6 beams and cut the

Project 9 Materials List

Description	Quantity	Length in feet	Comments
4×4	4	10	Posts
4×6	2	8	Beams
2×4	17	6	Stringers, bench tops
2×4	11	8	Table, bench supports
Lattice	2		4×8 prefabricated
1×1		72	Inner stops
Machine bolts	8		½"×7½" with nuts and washers
Carriage bolts	8		⅜"×5½" with nuts and washers
Carriage bolts	12		⅜"×3½" with nuts and washers
1¼" screws			As needed
2½" screws			As needed
8d nails			As needed
4d nails			As needed
Fence clips	4		As needed
1¼" angles	20		
3" angles	4		
Concrete mix	4		Sacks

bevels (optional) on the ends as shown in Figure 9.3. Set the beams on the ledgers and tack them in place with 8d nails. Then lay out the ½-inch-diameter holes as shown. Bore the holes through the posts and beams. Unless you have a long enough bit, you will have to do this in two operations, boring through the posts to mark the points on the beams, then moving the beams aside to complete the bores. Bolt the beams to the posts with ½ × 7½-inch machine bolts with washers. Remove the temporary ledgers.

Next, mount the 72-inch 2 × 4 stringers to the beams. You can toe-nail them in place or use 1¼-inch angles as shown in Figure 9.4.

MAKING THE BENCHES

The tops of the bench supports are 79½ inches from the tops of the posts, or 16½ inches from the ground. Cut four 2 × 4 bench supports 21½ inches long, and lop the corners at a 45-degree angle as shown in Figure 9.1. Bolt them in place with ⅜ × 5½-inch carriage bolts as shown in Figure 9.5. Make sure each support is level. Next, from 2 × 4 stock, cut four braces 20¼ inches long. Cut each end at a 45-degree angle. Bolt the braces to the supports with ⅜ × 3½-inch carriage bolts. Use a 3-inch angle with 1¼-inch screws to secure the braces to the posts, as shown in Figure 9.5.

For each bench, cut five 2 × 4s 55 inches long. Space them about ⅛ inch apart, and fasten them in place with 1¼-inch screws. A sixth 2 × 4 cut 48 inches long fits between the posts and forms the bottom rail of the trellis (see Figure 9.2).

Cut two 2 × 4 cleats 21 inches long, and mount them to the bench bottoms as shown.

INSTALLING THE LATTICE

The lattice is cut from prefabricated 48 × 96-inch panels. Cut each of them 60 inches long. Mount the top rails 60 inches above the bottom rails, and secure them with fence clips as shown in Figure 9.6.

Working from the center, lay out the 1 × 1 inner stops around the perimeter. Nail them in place with 4d galvanized nails about every 12 inches. Put the lattice in place, then nail on the outer stops.

MAKING THE TABLE

Refer to Figures 9.7, 9.8, and 9.9 for table details. All table components are made from 2 × 4 stock.

Begin by cutting four legs 32¾ inches long with parallel 30-degree angles on each end. Now lay out the half-laps, which also are at 30-degree angles as shown in Figure 9.9. Set your circular saw or radial arm saw to ¾ inch and make several passes through the waste area. Clean up the cuts with a sharp chisel. Use two 1¼-inch screws to hold each assembly together.

Cut a pair of table supports 24 inches long as shown. Cut seven 2 × 4s 48 inches long for the tabletop. Start with the center board and work outward, spacing each about ⅛ inch apart. Secure each one to the supports with two 1¼-inch screws at each end. Make sure that the supports are perpendicular to the top boards and the top is square. Turn the top assembly over, and mount a cleat in the bottom center of the top. With the table still upside down, bolt the leg assemblies to the top with ⅜ × 3½-inch carriage bolts. Finish the table by cutting a pair of 45-degree braces 20⅛ inches long and mounting them with 2½-inch screws.

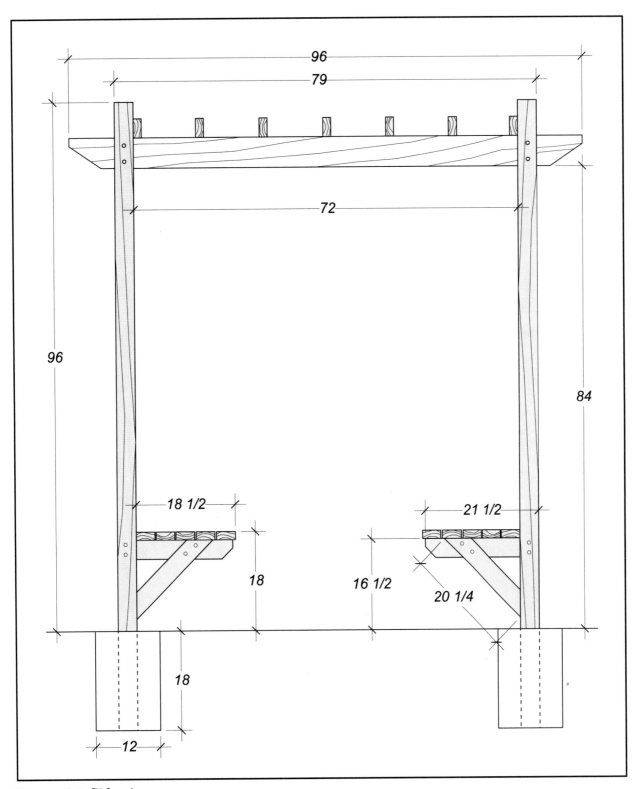

Figure 9.1. Side view

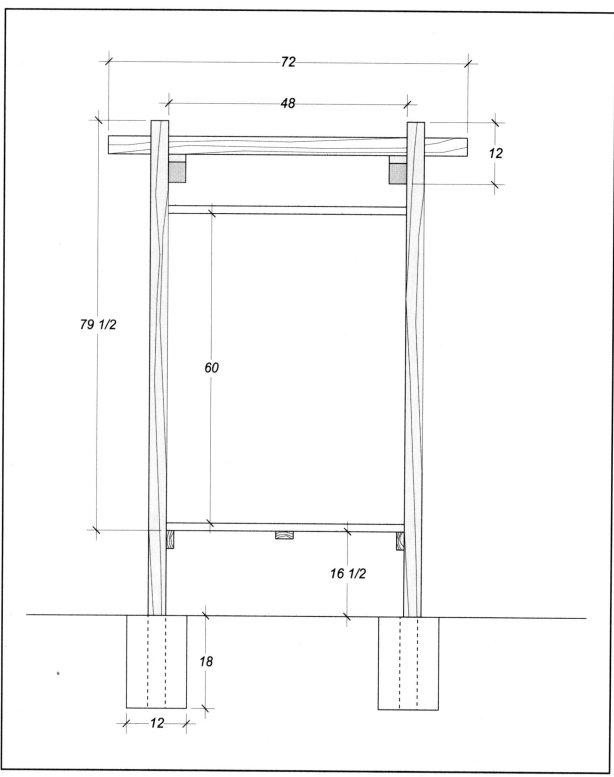

Figure 9.2. End view. Temporary ledgers hold the beams in place during installation.

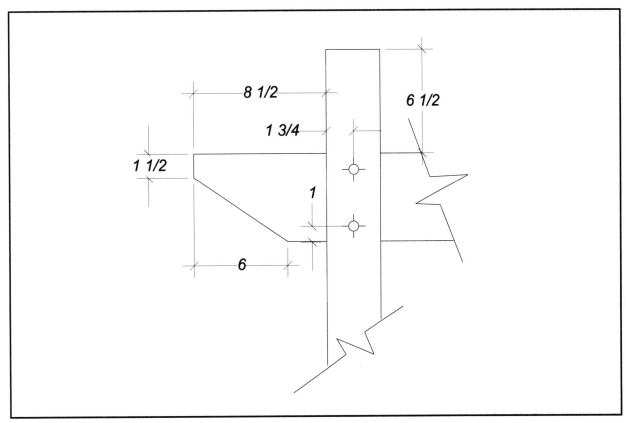

Figure 9.3. Bolt layout and bevel on beam end

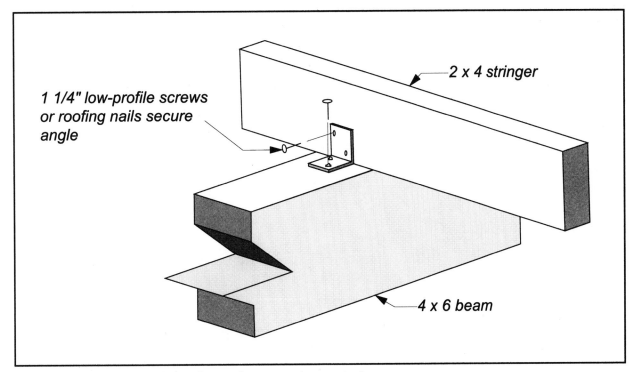

Figure 9.4. Use 1¼-inch angles to fasten stringers to beams

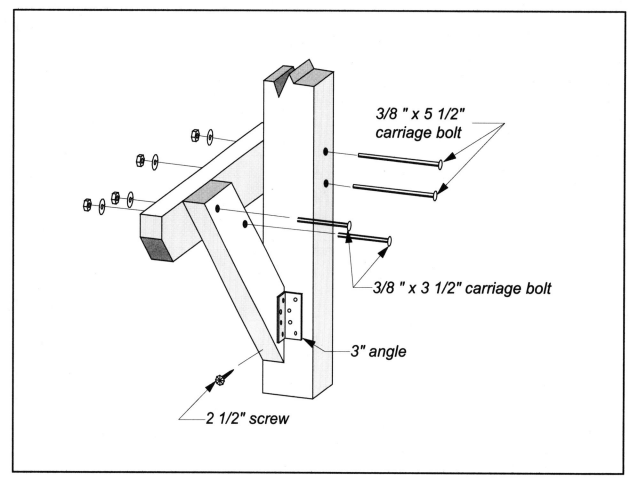

Figure 9.5. Bench support detail

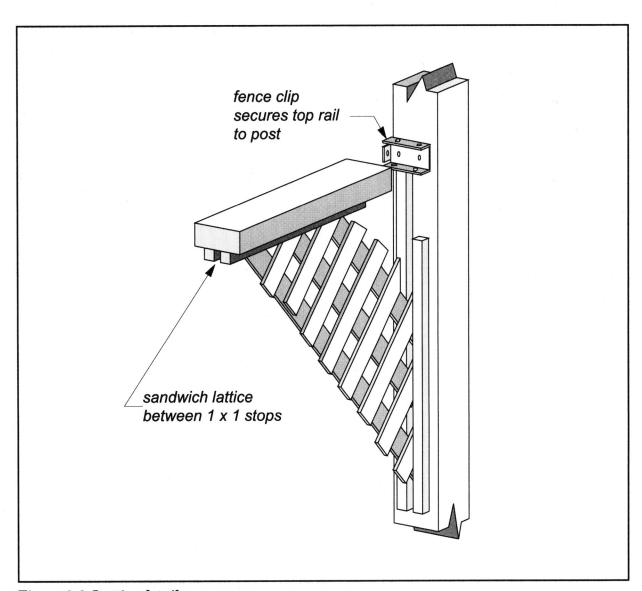

*fence clip
secures top rail
to post*

*sandwich lattice
between 1 x 1 stops*

Figure 9.6. Lattice detail

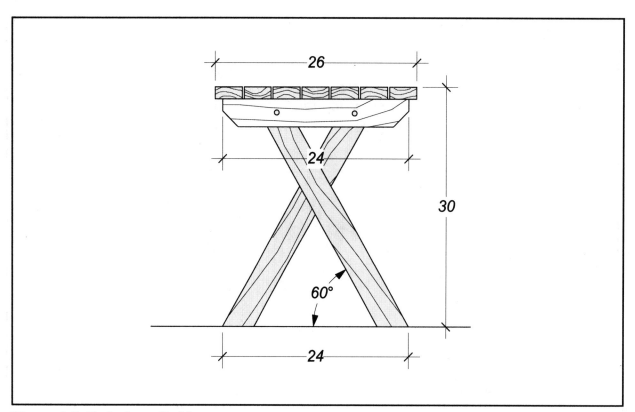

Figure 9.7. End view of table

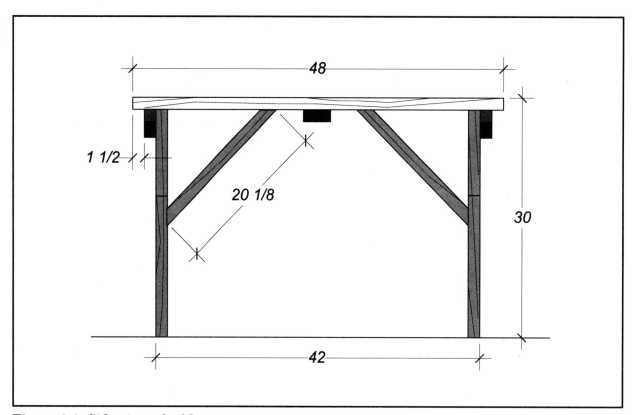

Figure 9.8. Side view of table

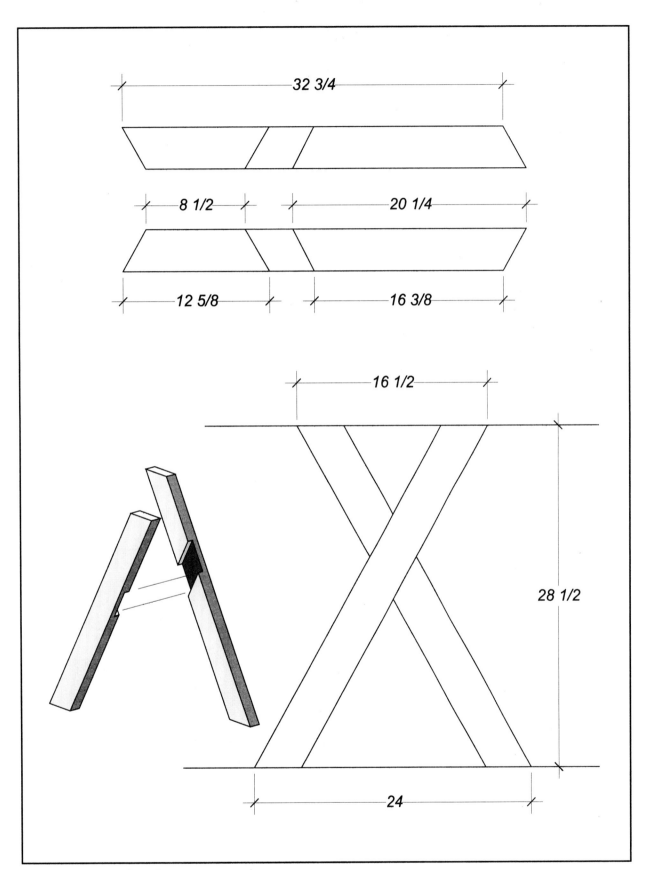

Figure 9.9. Leg detail

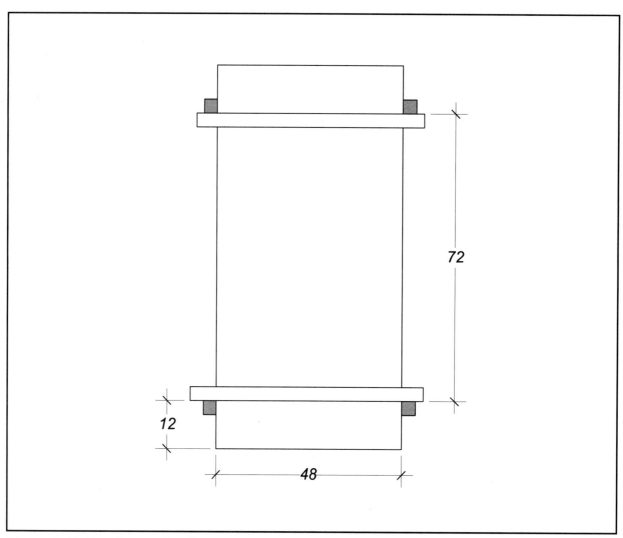

Figure 9.10. Post layout jig. Screw a pair of 2×4s to a sheet of ½-inch plywood. After digging the holes, place the jig on the ground and brace the posts firmly. Remove jig and recheck all dimensions at ground level and near the tops of the posts. Also recheck that the posts are plumb before pouring concrete.

ADIRONDACK CHAIR WITH WHEELS

What would a country garden be without an Adirondack chair or two? This classic is just right when you want to relax with a cold drink on a hot night. Its low-slung design lends itself to quite a few variations. Here's one with a twist—wheels on the front legs to make it easy to move.

MAKING THE LEG ASSEMBLY
Cut the front legs and seat supports as shown in Figure 10.3. The front legs are cut from 2×4 stock, and the seat supports are cut from 1×6 stock. Bore a 1⅛-inch-diameter hole in each leg. (Note: If you prefer to build a chair without wheels, add 1½

Project 10 Materials List

Description	Quantity	Length in feet	Comments
1×6	2	8	Seat supports, apron, arms
2×4	1	4	Legs
1×4	2	8	Seat slats, lower back support
1×3	4	6	Back slats, main back support, upper back support
¾" plywood	4		Square feet, wheels
1" dowel	1	4	Axle
¼" dowel			As needed for axle pins
1¼" screws			As needed
1½" screws			As needed
2½" screws			As needed

inches to the bottom of the legs.) The apron is a 1×6 cut 24 inches long. The lower back support, 21 inches long, is a 1×4 cut with a 10-degree bevel on one edge (see Figure 10.3).

Begin the leg assembly by mounting the apron into position on the front legs with three 1½-inch screws on each end as shown in Figure 10.4. Temporarily fasten a 2×4 to the bottom of the front legs to bring the front of the chair up to the correct height.

Use 1½-inch screws to attach the seat supports to the insides of the legs, keeping the upper edges of the supports flush with the top edge of the apron.

Attach the lower back support to the seat supports 15¼ inches down from the front legs.

ASSEMBLING THE ARMS, BACK, AND SEAT

Using the dimensions shown in Figure 10.3, cut the arms from 1×6 stock and cut the brackets and main back support from 1×3 stock. Also cut a length of 1×4 (or equivalent) 17¾ inches long to prop up the arm assembly during installation.

Begin the arm assembly by mounting the arm brackets to the legs with two 2½-inch screws each. Now, with the arms upside down, mount the main back support on the ends of the arms with 1¼-inch screws. Carefully turn the arm assembly right side up and place it on the legs, with the prop holding up the back end. Referring to Figures 10.1 and 10.2, check the alignment, and secure the arms to the legs and brackets with 1½-inch screws.

Cut the 1×3 slats for the back as shown in Figure 10.3. Mount the center slat first, flush with the bottom of the lower support, and attach with one 1¼-inch screw into the upper and lower supports each. Then use a single screw at the bottom to mount the remaining slats, placing them about ½ inch apart. Now fan the slats, and screw them to the main support.

The upper back support is a 1×3 cut 24 inches long. Mount it 4 inches below the tops of the shortest slats.

To make the seat, cut four 1×4s 24 inches long, and one 21 inches long to fit between the legs. Mount that one first, flush with the front of the apron, using two 1¼-

inch screws at each end. Evenly space the remainder of the seat slats down the slope of the seat supports, and screw them in place.

MAKING AND INSTALLING THE WHEELS

Make the 8-inch-diameter wheels out of ¾-inch plywood. You will need a little less than 4 square feet—that is, four pieces about 9 inches square. Glue two pieces together to make each of the two blanks. Use waterproof glue and clamp the pieces together until dry.

Locate the center of each blank and scribe a circle. Use a band saw or saber saw to cut the blanks just outside the line. Use a power sander (a table-mounted disk sander

is best) to smooth up the wheels. Bore a 1-inch-diameter hole through the center of each wheel.

The axle is a piece of 1-inch diameter dowel cut 30 inches long. To locate the pins to hold the wheels in place, first find the center of the axle. Make the ¼-inch hardwood dowel. The pins should be 2 inches long. Measure outward half the width of the chair (12 inches). Add to this the thickness of the wheel plus ¼ inch (⅛ inch for space between the wheel and leg plus the radius of the pin). At this point, bore ¼-inch holes perpendicular to the grain.

Slip one wheel onto the axle just past the pinhole. Tap in the pin, and pull the wheel back tight against it. Slip the axle through the legs, and put on the other wheel.

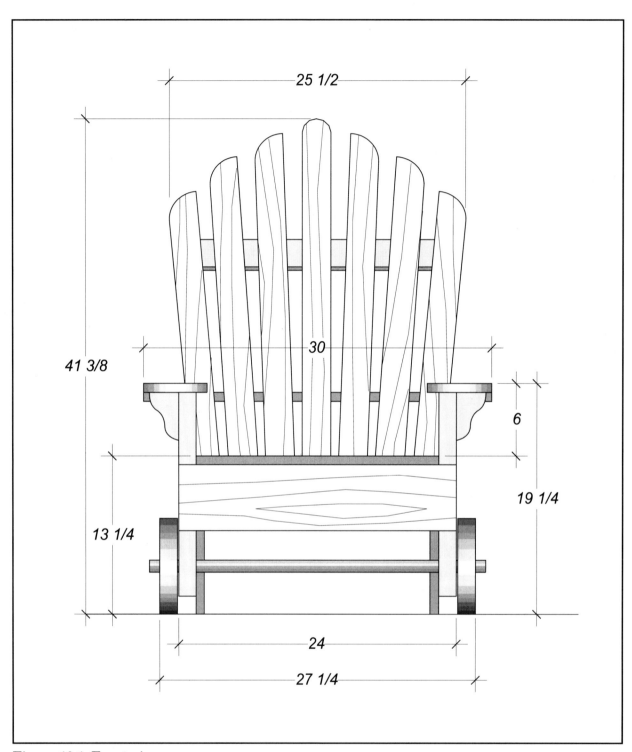

Figure 10.1. Front view

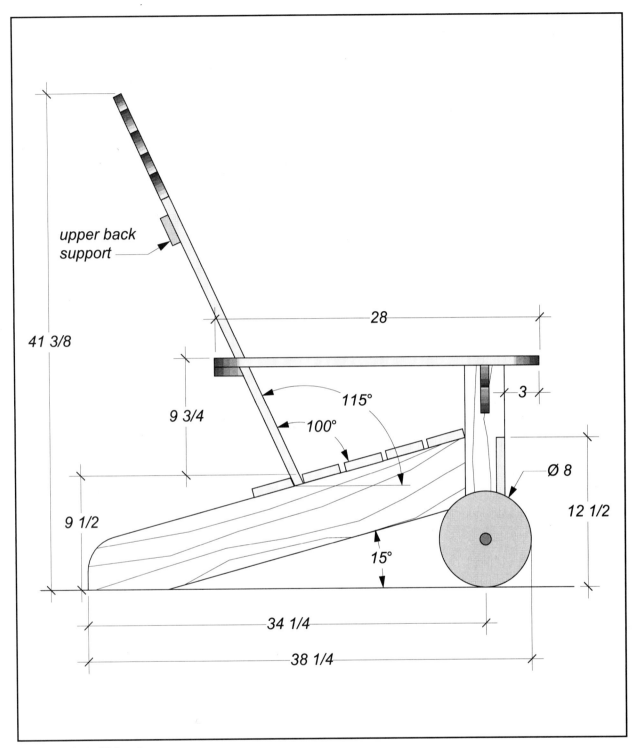

Figure 10.2. Side view

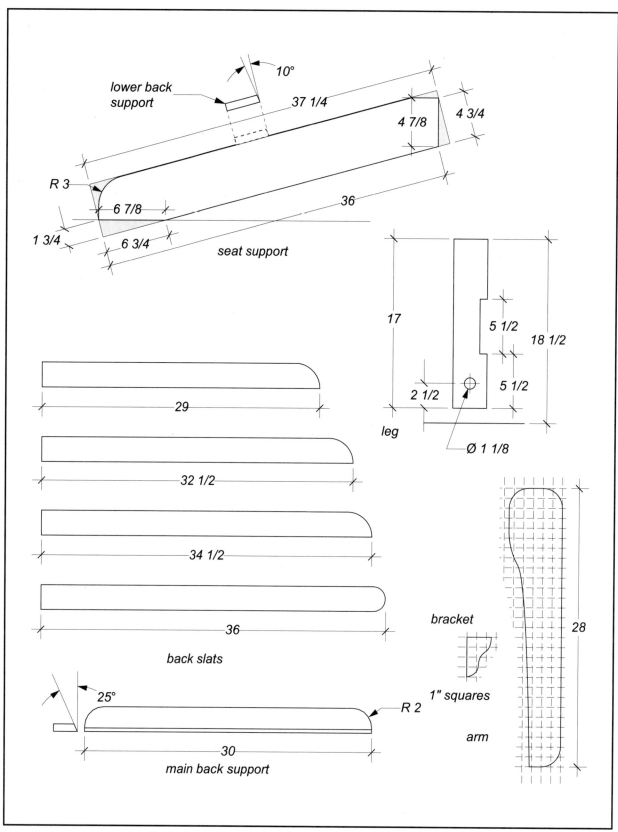

Figure 10.3. Patterns and dimensions for seat supports, legs, back slats, lower and main back supports, arms, and arm brackets

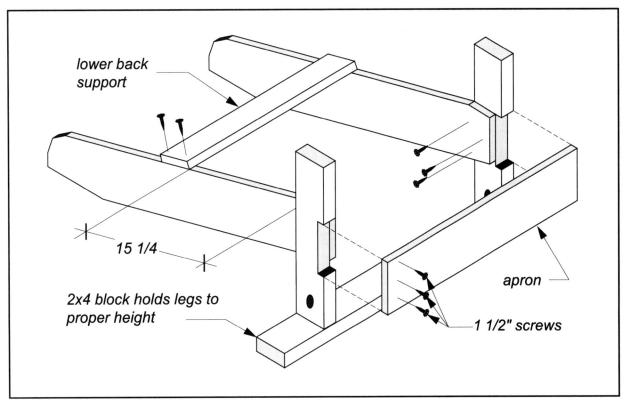

Figure 10.4. Leg assembly detail

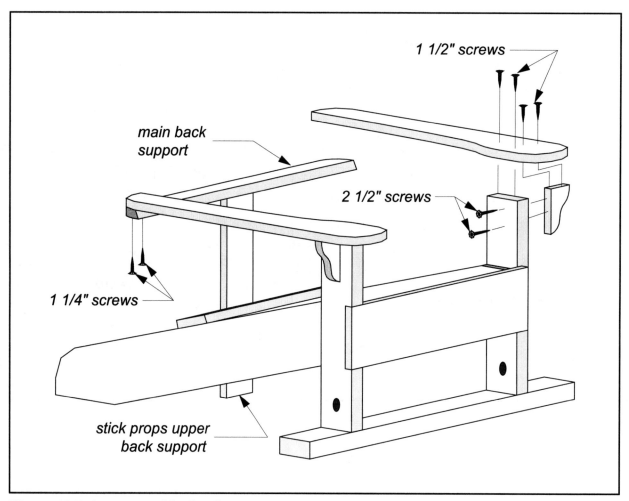

Figure 10.5. Arm assembly detail

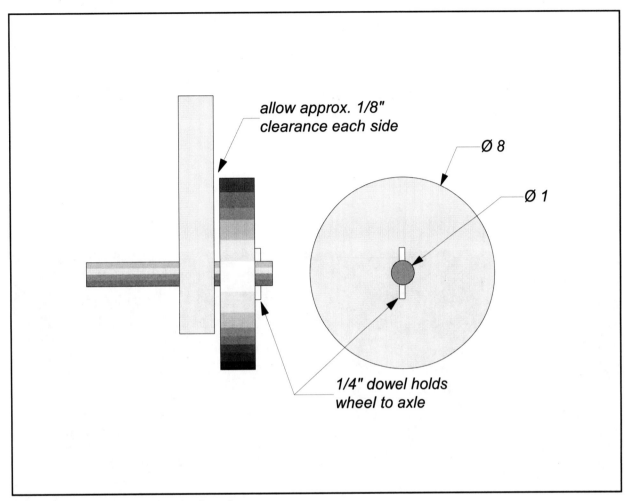

allow approx. 1/8"
clearance each side

Ø 8

Ø 1

1/4" dowel holds
wheel to axle

Figure 10.6. Wheel and axle detail

▪ Project 11 ▪

GARDEN BENCH

Set this garden bench under a shady tree, and you'll have a good place to take a break from pulling weeds and cultivating the pole beans. The bench is sturdy yet relatively easy to build and offers comfort as well as a pleasing form.

MAKING THE BACK

The back is composed of a 2×6 top rail, a 2×4 bottom rail, and seven 1-inch-diameter spindles. Both rails have a ½-inch long tenon on each end (see Figure 11.5). The spindles are set into holes bored ⁹⁄₁₆ inches deep.

Begin by cutting the rails 46 inches long. Lay out the tenons, making sure that the distance between the shoulders is the same for both rails (45 inches).

Now, cut the tenons. It is easiest to cut these with a radial arm saw, but you can also cut them by hand with a back saw.

Working from the center of each rail, lay out the spindles. Then bore the holes $9/16$-inch deep, being careful that they are on the mark and perpendicular to the surface.

Now cut the curve in the top rail (Figure 11.4) with a band saw or saber saw, then sand the cut smooth.

Cut the spindles 11 inches long, and cut two 1×2 (or equivalent) spacers 10 inches long.

Put a dab of construction adhesive in the bottom of each hole (the extra $1/16$ inch is to accommodate the adhesive). Then put the spindles and rails together with a spacer between the rails at each end. Use a pair of bar clamps to hold the assembly until the adhesive has set.

MAKING THE LEGS

Each leg assembly is composed of a front leg, rear leg, and seat support. The front legs are 2×4s cut 24 inches long. The rear legs are cut from 2×6s and are 34 inches long. The three seat supports are made from 2×4s and are $22\frac{3}{4}$ inches long. Refer to Figure 11.4 for the patterns for the rear legs and seat supports.

The next step is to bolt the seat supports to the legs with $\frac{1}{4} \times 3\frac{1}{2}$-inch carriage bolts (see Figure 11.3 for layout details). Make sure that the front and rear legs are parallel and that the seat support is perpendicular to them. Unbolt the rear legs from their seat supports.

Now lay out the mortises on the insides of each rear leg according to the dimensions given in Figure 11.5. Use a 1-inch bit to bore out most of the waste material, then finish the mortises with a sharp chisel. As you go along, check the fit of the tenons on the seat back.

ASSEMBLING THE SEAT AND ARMS

Once you've achieved a good fit, use two $2\frac{1}{2}$-inch screws at each mortise-and-tenon joint to hold the rear legs to the back. Then rebolt the leg assemblies together.

Cut the 1×4 rear apron 45 inches long and mount it to the rear ends of the seat supports with $1\frac{1}{2}$-inch screws.

Rip the front apron $2\frac{3}{4}$ inches wide with a 12-degree bevel (see inset, Figure 11.6). Cut it $46\frac{1}{2}$ inches long. Mount it to the front ends of the seat supports. Notice in Figure 11.1 that the apron extends beyond the seat supports but not to the outer edges of the legs.

Project 11 Materials List

Description	Quantity	Length in feet	Comments
2×6	1	10	Rear legs, top rail
2×4	2	8	Front legs, arms, seat supports, bottom rail
1×2	6	8	Seat slats
1×4	1	8	Front apron, rear apron
1" dowel	2	4	Spindles
Carriage bolts	10		$\frac{1}{4}" \times 3\frac{1}{2}"$ with nuts and washers
$1\frac{1}{2}"$ screws			As needed
$2\frac{1}{2}"$ screws			As needed

Before securing the apron, make sure that the outside-to-outside distance across the front of the bench is the same as that across the back (48 inches).

Center the middle seat support between the aprons, and secure it with 1½-inch screws.

Then, for the seat slats, cut 1×2 stock 46½ inches long. Next cut the two slats that fit between the legs 45 inches long. Notch the first and last one around the legs as necessary.

Cut the arms out of 2×4 stock according to the pattern shown in Figure 11.4. Mount them with 2½-inch screws as shown in Figure 11.6.

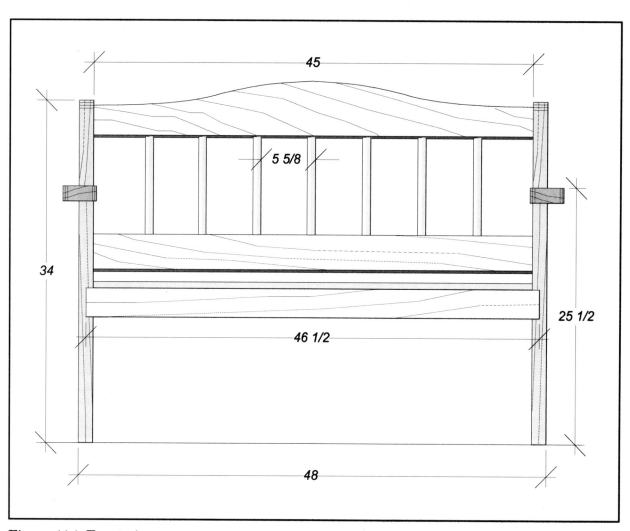

Figure 11.1. Front view

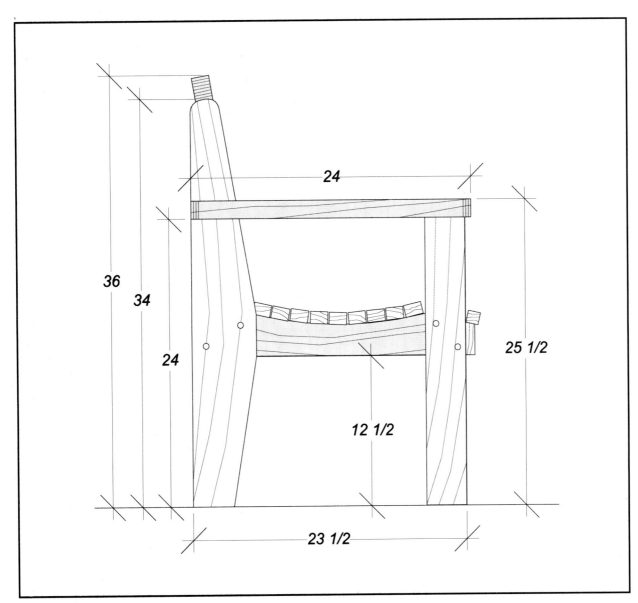

Figure 11.2. End view

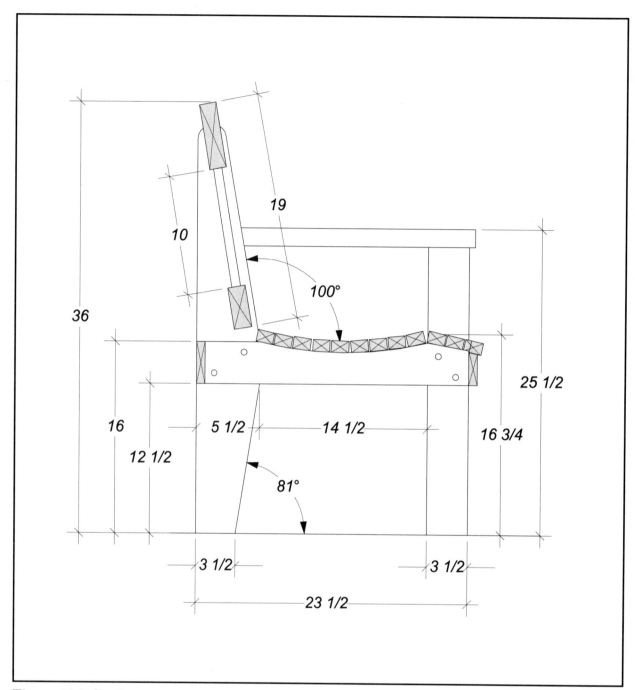

Figure 11.3. Section

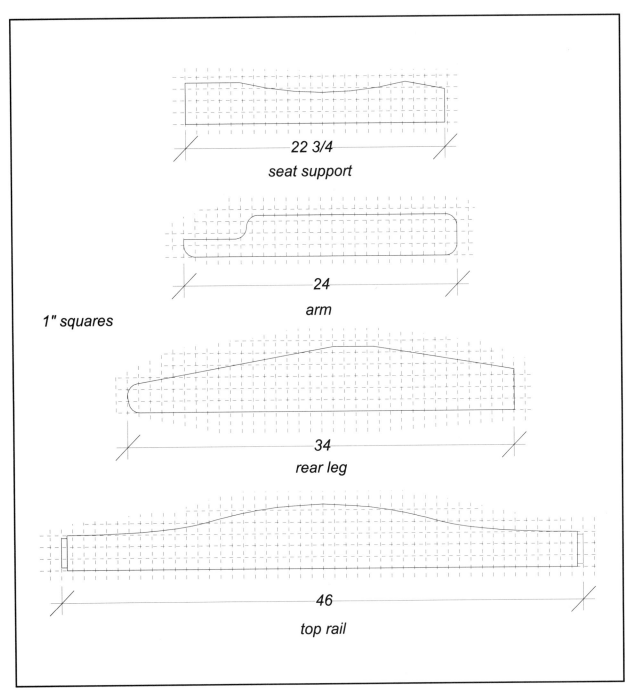

Figure 11.4. Patterns for seat supports, arms, rear legs, and top rail

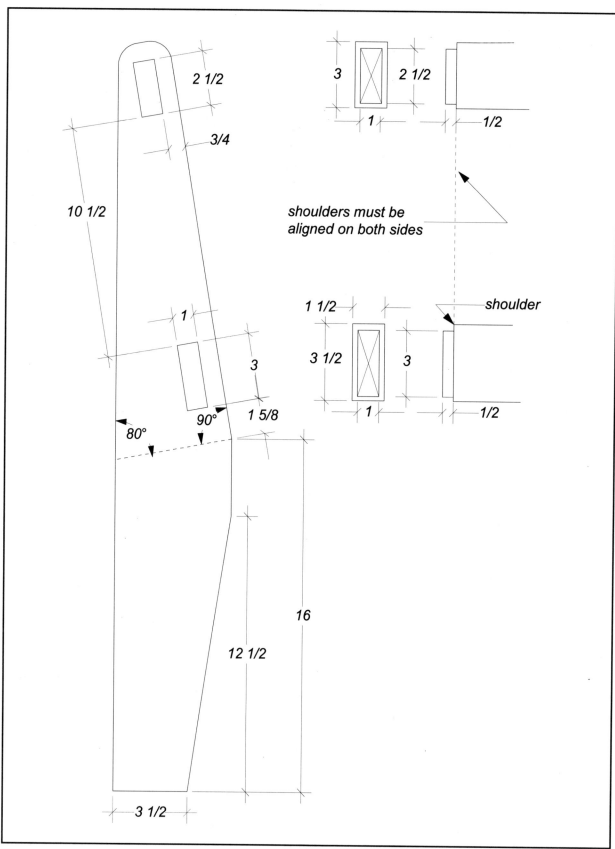

Figure 11.5. Mortise and tenon detail

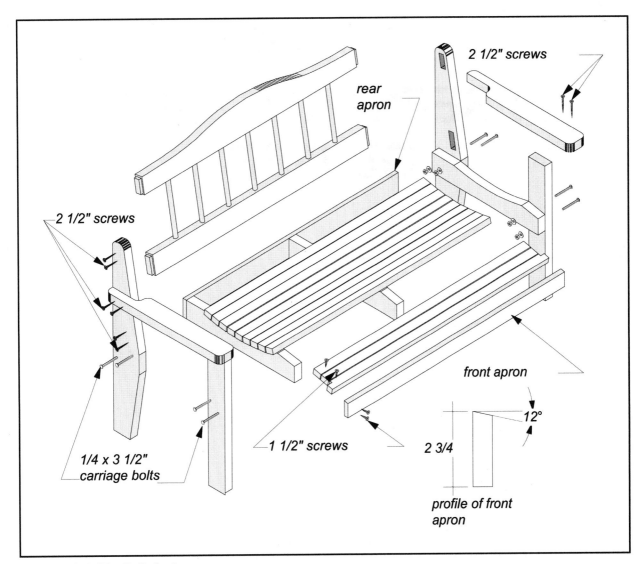

2 1/2" screws

rear apron

2 1/2" screws

front apron

1/4 x 3 1/2" carriage bolts

1 1/2" screws

2 3/4

12°

profile of front apron

Figure 11.6. Exploded view

▪ Project 12 ▪

FREESTANDING GLIDER

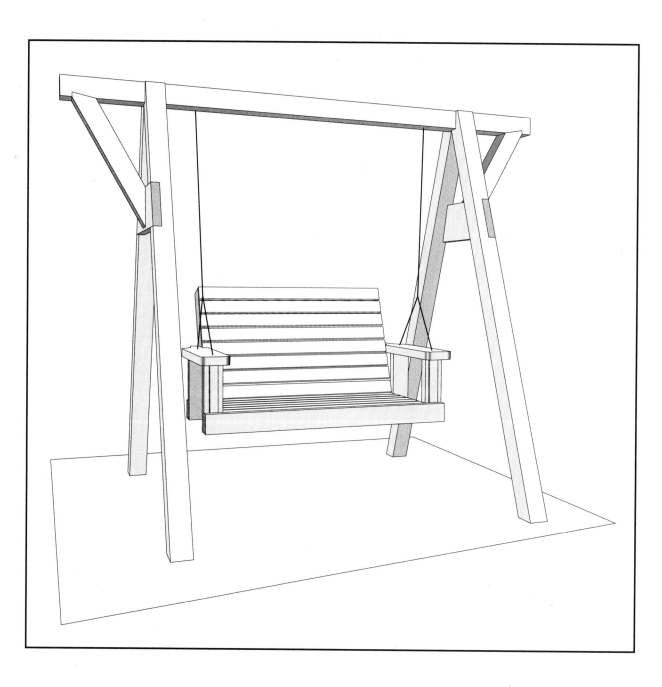

What could be more relaxing than swinging gently in the company of a good friend with stars overhead and crickets chirping in the background? The support structure for this freestanding glider is sturdy yet portable, so you can put it just about anywhere. If you have a porch with a substantial overhang, you can hang the glider there.

MAKING THE SUPPORT STRUCTURE

The support structure is made almost entirely of 4×4 stock. Cut four 4×4 legs 80½ inches long with 20-degree angles on both ends, as shown in Figure 12.2.

The main beam fits into seat cuts made in the posts, as shown in Figure 12.3.

Carefully lay out the bolts that will hold the beam to the legs. Use a 1½-inch-diameter spade bit to make a counterbore that will provide a flat surface on which the washers will seat. Now bore a 9/16-inch-diameter hole through each counterbore, making sure they are in proper alignment with each other.

The 2×8 leg braces are recessed into the legs. To locate them, lay the legs on a flat surface, their seat cuts together at the top and their bottoms 60⅞ inches apart as shown. Temporarily tack 1×4s (or equivalent) at the top and bottom of the assembly to hold it together.

Use a straightedge across both legs to mark the top and bottom edges of the brace. Use a circular saw set 1½ inches deep to make several passes through the waste area. Knock out the waste, and clean up the cuts with a chisel.

Cut a length of 2×8 and check the fit.

Project 12 Materials List

Description	Quantity	Length in feet	Comments
4×4	6	8	Support structure
2×8	1	4	Leg braces
2×4	3	8	Glider frame
2×6	1	6	Arms
1×3	7	8	Slats
Machine bolts	2		½"×6" with nuts and washers
Eyebolts	2		½"×4" with nuts and washers
Eyebolts	4		⅜"×14" with nuts and washers
Carriage bolts	8		5/16"×3½" with nuts and washers
Carriage bolts	2		⅜"×4" with nuts and washers
1¼" screws			As needed
2½" screws			As needed
3" screws			As needed
3½" screws			As needed
Chain		10	Minimum length needed
S hooks	6		

Fasten it to the legs with three 3-inch screws at each end. Then trim the brace to the legs.

Next, lay out the 8-foot 4×4 beam. Place the beam on a flat surface, and mark the position of the legs 14½ inches in from each end. Mark the bolt holes. Check that your layout corresponds with holes you've cut in the legs before boring the 9/16-inch-diameter holes.

Use a length of 4×4 or 2×4—to simulate the legs—and place it at right angles to the beam. Also lay out the braces on 4×4 stock as shown in Figure 12.4. Note that each brace fits into a seat cut on the underside of the beam. When everything checks out, cut the braces and make seat cuts.

Finally, bore the ½-inch-diameter holes for the eyebolts that will carry the glider.

RAISING THE SUPPORT STRUCTURE

Lift one of the leg assemblies at its peak high enough to cradle one end of the beam. Loosely bolt the beam in place with a ½×6-inch machine bolt. Temporarily brace the beam and leg assembly at right angles to one another, then mount the brace as shown in Figure 12.4. Tighten the bolt. Repeat the process at the other end. Make sure that the measurements between the legs are consistent and that both leg assemblies are at right angles to the beam. Install the ½×4-inch eyebolts.

MAKING THE GLIDER

Begin the glider by making the bench frame as shown in Figure 12.5. Rip the slat supports from 2×4 stock 2¾ inches wide. Secure them to the 2×4 rails with 2½-inch screws.

Next, cut four 2×4 arm supports 12 inches long. Make a ½×½-inch dado down the center of each, as shown in Figure 12.6, to accommodate the 3/8×14-inch eyebolts that will support the glider. It's important that the glider be supported from the bottom; do not attach the chain to the arms themselves. If you can't find eyebolts of sufficient length to go through the arms and their supports, run the chain all the way through and bolt it to the bottom of the glider. In this case, make the dadoes wide enough to accommodate the chain. Now bolt the arm supports to the rails with 5/16×3½-inch carriage bolts.

Cut three back supports out of 2×4 stock as shown in Figure 12.6. Mount them to the rear rail, directly behind the seat supports, with 2½-inch screws. Offset the screws from the screws already through the back rail.

Out of 2×6 stock, cut a pair of arms according to the pattern shown in Figure 12.7. The pattern also shows the layout of the 3/8-inch diameter holes for the 3/8×14-inch eyebolts and their relationship to the arm supports. Use the eyebolts to locate and secure the arms to their supports. Don't forget the washers on the upper ends of the bolts. Use a 3/8×4-inch carriage bolt to hold each arm to its back support. Further secure the arms to their supports with two 2½-inch screws at each support.

Cut fourteen 1×3 slats 41 inches long, and mount them to the seat and back supports with 1¼-inch screws, one driven into each of the supports.

Chain comes in several configurations and strengths. Consult your hardware dealer regarding suitable chain. Use S hooks to fasten the chain to the eyebolts. Cut two lengths of chain about 24 inches long and attach them to the glider arms. Attach the main chains to the shorter lengths and to the beam. Experiment with the length and placement of the main chain for a comfortable height and for the right degree of glider incline.

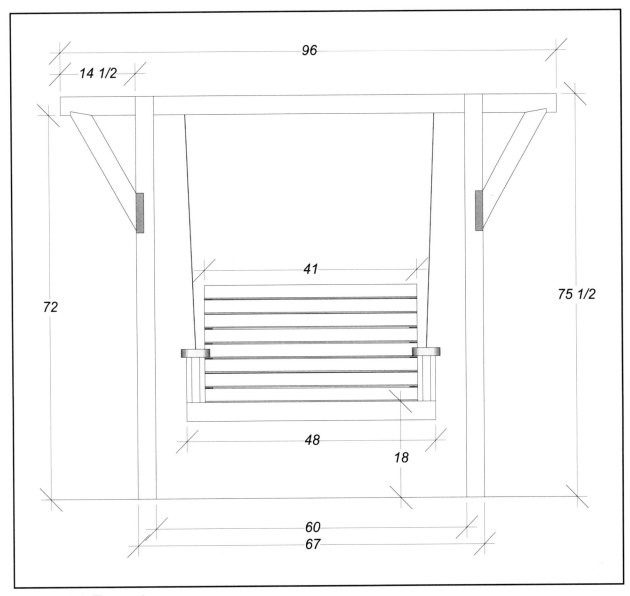

Figure 12.1. Front view

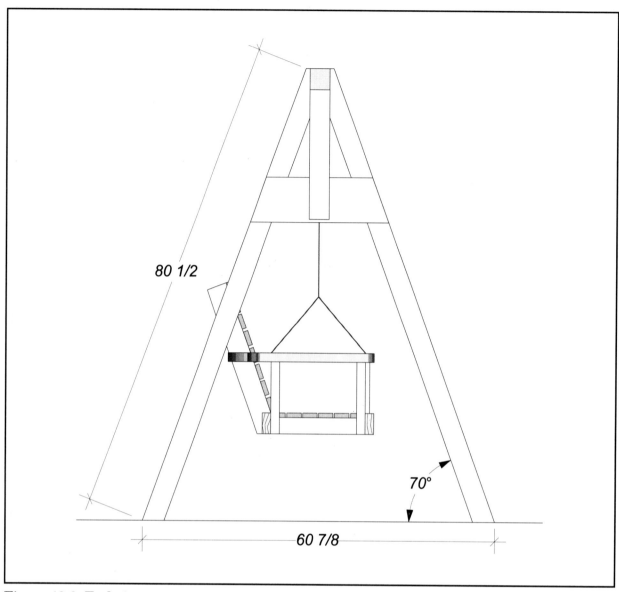

Figure 12.2. End view

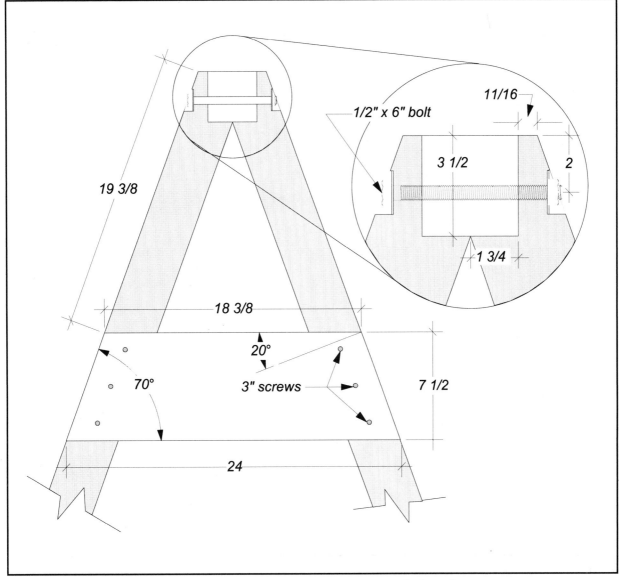

Figure 12.3. Detail of leg brace, beam seat cuts, and machine bolt at beam

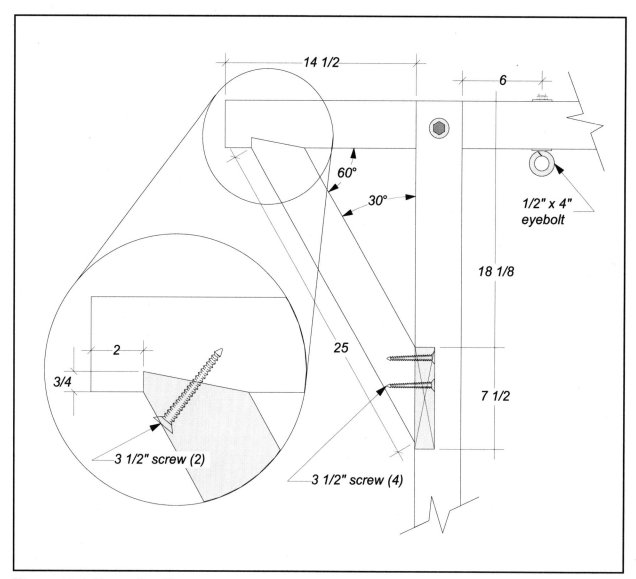

Figure 12.4. Brace detail

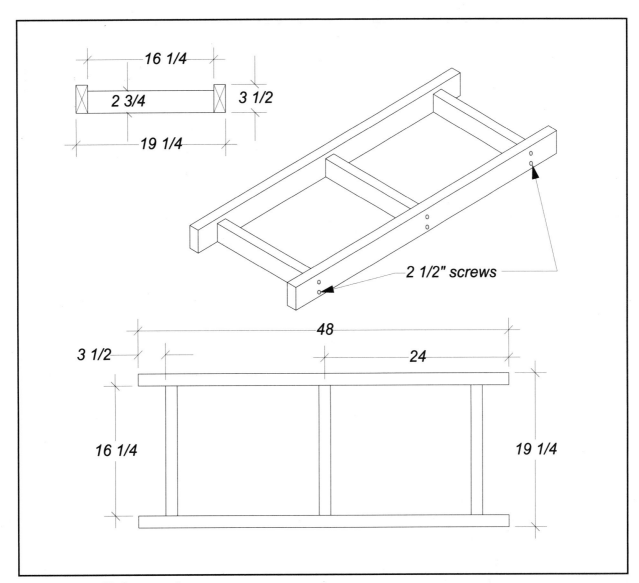

16 1/4

2 3/4   3 1/2

19 1/4

2 1/2" screws

48

3 1/2   24

16 1/4   19 1/4

Figure 12.5. Glider seat frame

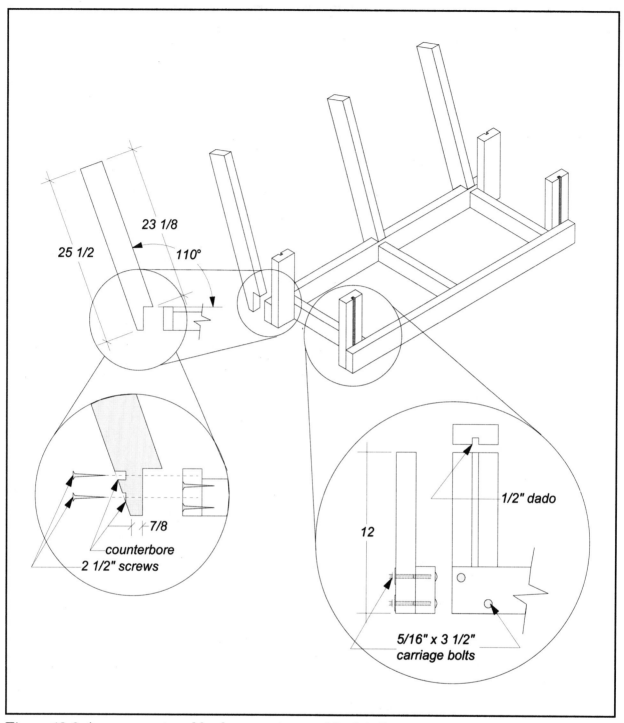

Figure 12.6. Arm support and back support assembly detail

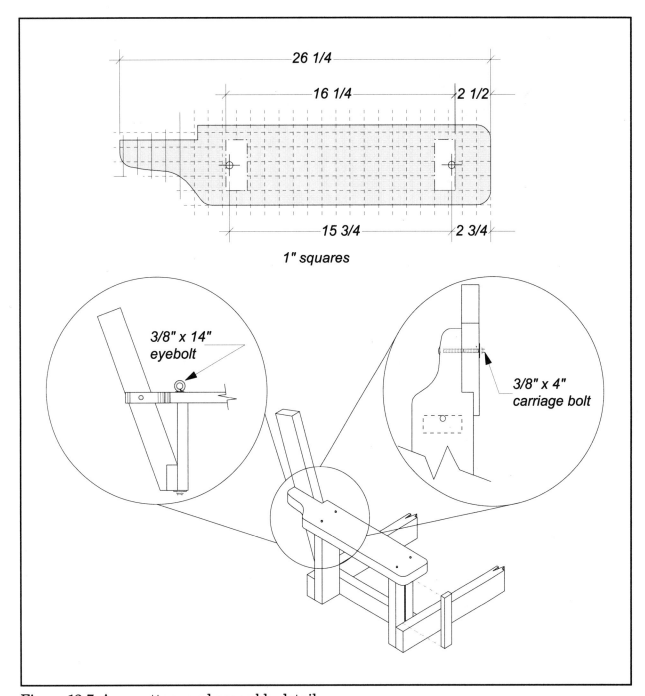

26 1/4

16 1/4   2 1/2

15 3/4   2 3/4

1" squares

3/8" x 14"
eyebolt

3/8" x 4"
carriage bolt

Figure 12.7. Arm pattern and assembly detail

▪ Project 13 ▪

ARCHED BRIDGE

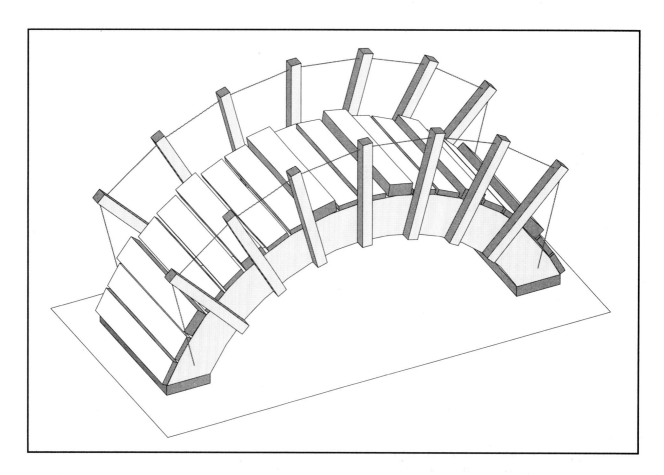

If you have a rock garden or small stream, this traditional arched bridge could be the perfect enhancement. Each arch is made of two pieces of ¾-inch AC plywood laminated together. The arches can be cut from a single sheet of plywood. You can make the bridge with or without the decorative railing, which is constructed of 2×2s strung with ½-inch-diameter nylon rope.

MAKING THE ARCHES

Refer to Figure 13.3 for the arch geometry. Make the pattern out of a sheet of ¼-inch plywood or a large sheet of heavy paper. The paper must be large enough to locate the center of a half-circle with a diameter of 65 inches (radius 32½ inches). To scribe the arcs, use a stick about 36 inches long. Drive a small nail near one end to use as a pivot

Project 13 Materials List

Description	Quantity	Length in feet	Comments
¾" plywood	1		Sheet, AC, arches
2×8	1	4	Footing blocks
2×6	1	10	Bridging blocks
2×4	1	12	Decking
1×4	4	8	Decking
2×2	5	8	Spindles
Joist hangers	6		2×6
Angle	4		1½"×4"
Nylon rope		20	½" diameter
1¼" screws			As needed
2½" screws			As needed
3" screws			As needed
Construction Adhesive			As needed

point. From that point, measure 26½ inches and 32½ inches, and bore holes the diameter of a pencil through the stick at these points. Draw the arcs by fixing a pencil into first one hole, then the other.

Note: If you plan to install the railing, you can lay out the spindles directly on the pattern for easy transfer to the finished arches (see "Adding the Railing").

Figure 13.4 shows how you can get four arch segments out of one sheet of plywood. Use a saber saw to cut out the arch pieces, cutting not quite to the line.

Pair up the pieces, choosing the two with the best surfaces for the outside. Apply a generous amount of construction adhesive or other waterproof glue to the inner surface of one of the outside pieces. Place its mate atop, and fasten them together with 1¼-inch screws placed about 8 inches apart and 1 inch in from the perimeter. Repeat the process for the other arch.

Once the adhesive has set, pare off any excess glue, then clamp or screw the two arches together and use a belt sander to achieve the final shape.

MAKING THE BRIDGE

Cut five 2×6 bridging blocks 17 inches long. With the arches still secured together, lay out the five bridging blocks as shown in Figure 13.5, one in the center of the arch, one each at the bottom, and one each between the two on both sides.

Now unclamp the arches and mount the bridging. Figure 13.5 illustrates how you can use 2×6 joist hangers and 1½×4-inch angles to mount the bridging. Alternatively, you can drive 3-inch screws through the outside of the arches into the bridging. Both methods are acceptable and will achieve the same results.

Finish the arch assembly by mounting a 2×8 20-inch footing at each end as shown.

The treads that form the bridge surface are made of 2×4s and 1×4s cut 20 inches long. Begin at the center with two 1×4s, and work your way down both sides, alternating one 2×4, two 1×4s, and so on as shown in Figure 13.6. For a different effect, experiment with 2×2s and 1×2s and vary the pattern. Use 1½-inch screws to mount the 1×4s and 2½-inch screws for the 2×4s, one screw centered at each end.

The flat surface of the treads will not match the curved surface of the arch. You can use a belt sander to modify the underside of each tread, or fill the voids with construction adhesive for a perfect, solid fit.

ADDING THE RAILING

Cut the fourteen 16-inch-long spindles out of 2×2 stock. Bore a ½-inch-diameter hole about 1 inch below the top of each spindle as shown in Figure 13.6. Also bore a hole near each footing as shown.

Use the pattern to lay out the spindles, and mount them flush with the bottom of the arch with two 2½-inch or 3-inch screws in each.

Knot one end of the rope on the inside of one of the arches and thread through the hole near the footing. Thread the rope through each spindle on one side, down through the hole at the other end of the arch, out the opposite side, and through the spindles on the other side. Pull the rope through the final hole in the arch, and knot on the inside.

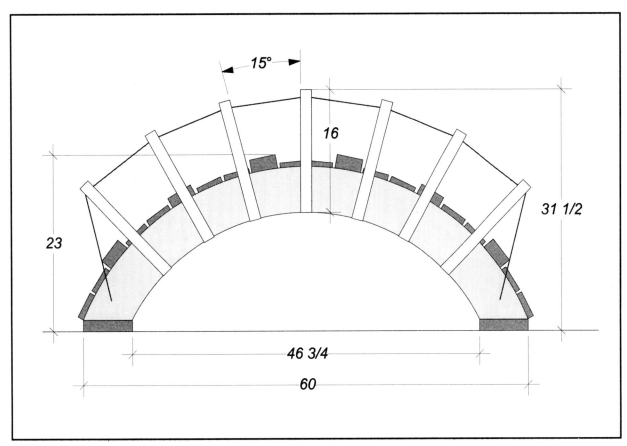

Figure 13.1 Side view

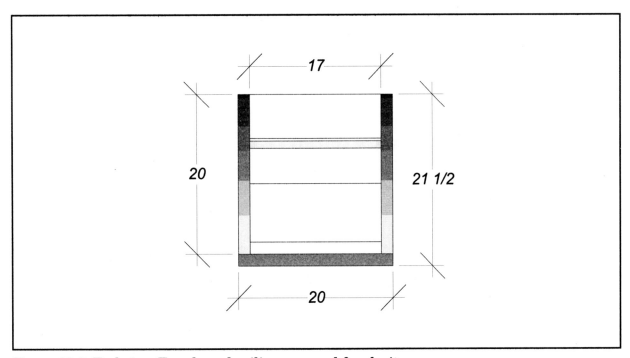

Figure 13.2. End view. Treads and railing removed for clarity

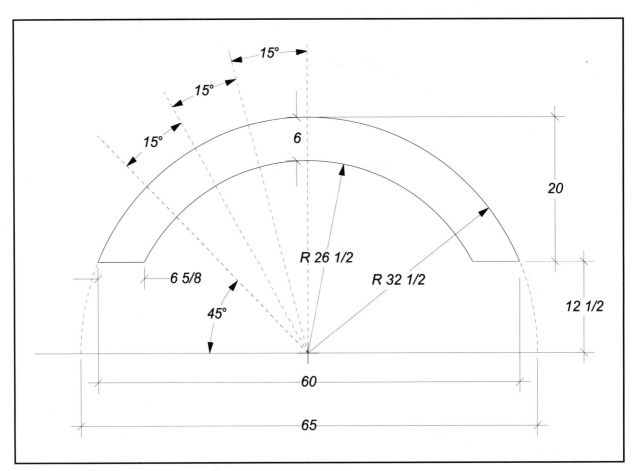

Figure 13.3. Arch geometry and pattern

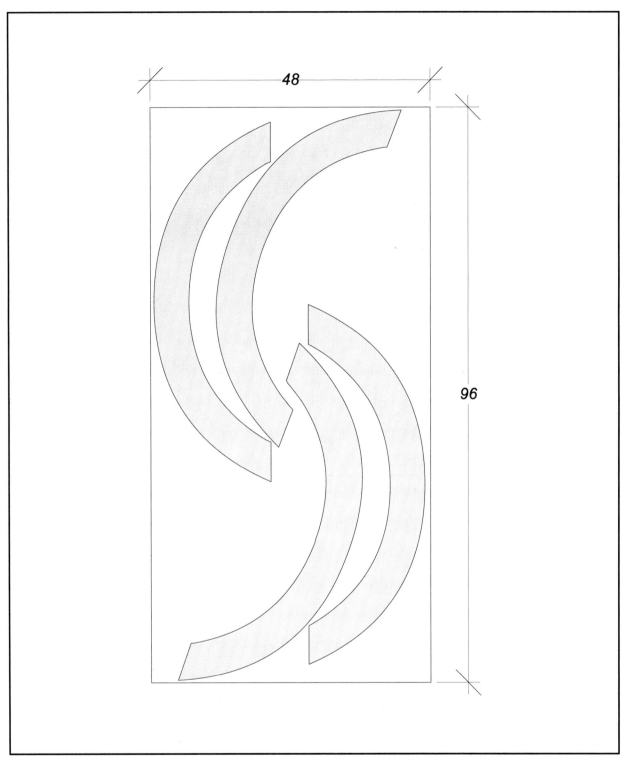

Figure 13.4. Cutting layout. You can get all four arch pieces out of a single sheet of ¾-inch plywood.

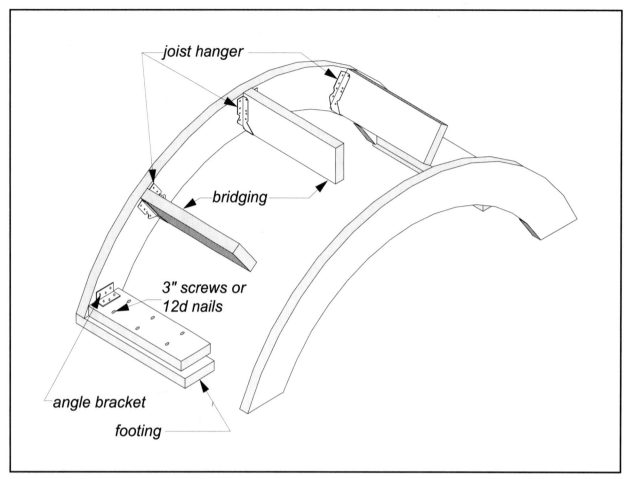

Figure 13.5. Exploded view of bridge structure

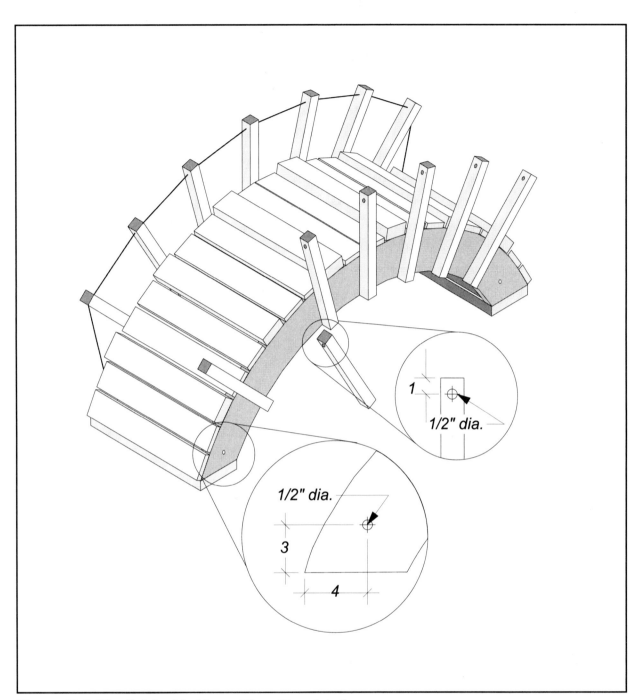

Figure 13.6. The finished bridge, with railing detail

▪ Project 14 ▪

POTTING BENCH

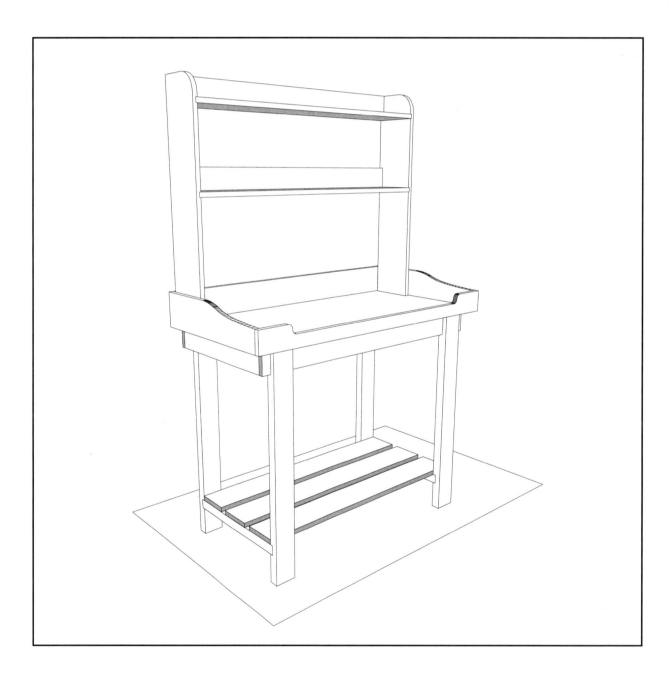

Every gardener needs a place to work—a place to mix soil and transplant seedlings. This potting bench offers lots of table and shelf space. Add hooks to the table and hutch sides to hang tools. The overall length of the table is 48 inches, but the design is suitable for lengths up to 96 inches. For longer lengths, you will need to add intermediate support in the table frame and beneath the bottom shelves, or use 2×6s instead of 1×6s. The table frame is made of 2×4s. Make the tabletop with ¾-inch AC plywood, with solid stock forming the rails. You can make the hutch out of plywood or solid stock.

MAKING THE TABLE

To make the table frame, cut the front and back frame rails 48 inches long, then make a ¾×1½-inch rabbet cut in each end as shown in Figure 14.3. Cut the side frame rails 20½ inches long. Assemble the frame with 2-inch screws. Make sure the frame is square.

Cut the 2×4 legs 35¼ inches long. Cut a ¾×1½-inch rabbet in the top end of each one. The back legs will fit on the inside of the table frame and the front legs on the outside. Keeping this in mind, cut a ½-inch-deep dado in each leg for the 2×4 stretchers

as shown in Figure 14.3. Check the fit of the stretchers, which are 20 inches long, before proceeding.

Now turn the table frame upside down and mount the legs, using three 1½-inch screws as shown. Before driving the screws, make sure the legs are at right angles to the frame.

Then slip the stretchers into place and secure them with a pair of 2-inch screws at each end as shown.

Turn the table right side up, and secure the 41-inch 1×6 shelving (or equivalent) to the stretchers with 1½-inch screws, two at each end of each shelf section.

To make the tabletop, cut a piece of ¾-inch AC plywood 46½ inches long and 22½ inches wide. Next, out of 1×6 stock, cut the front, back, and side rails as shown in the patterns in Figure 14.4. Attach the rails to the table with 1½-inch screws driven about 8 inches apart. Use two screws in each front corner and three screws in each back corner to hold the rails together. Screw the tabletop directly to the frame to complete the table.

MAKING THE HUTCH

To make the hutch, first cut two 36-inch-long pieces of 1×8. Cut two ¼-inch-deep

Project 14 Materials List

Description	Quantity	Length in feet	Comments
2×4	4	8	Table frame
1×6	3	8	Bottom shelves, table rails
1×8	2	8	Hutch sides, shelves
1×4	1	8	Hutch shelf backs
¾" plywood	8		Square feet, AC, tabletop
1¼" screws			As needed
1½" screws			As needed
2" screws			As needed

dadoes on the inside of each as shown in Figure 14.5. Then round the upper front corners with a 3-inch radius.

Cut two 1×8 shelves 45½ inches and two 1×4 shelf backs 45 inches long.

Fasten the shelves in the dadoes with 1¼-inch screws, three at each end. Slip the backs into place, and drive two 1½-inch screws into each through the sides. Then drive a minimum of four 1½-inch screws through the bottom of each shelf into its back.

Finally, mount the hutch to the table with four 1¼-inch screws driven through the inside face of the hutch sides into the table side rails.

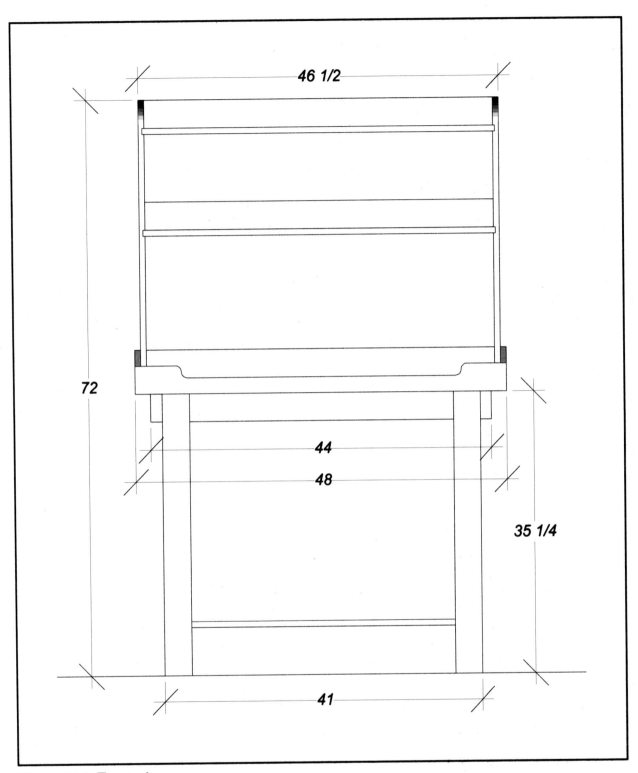

Figure 14.1. Front view

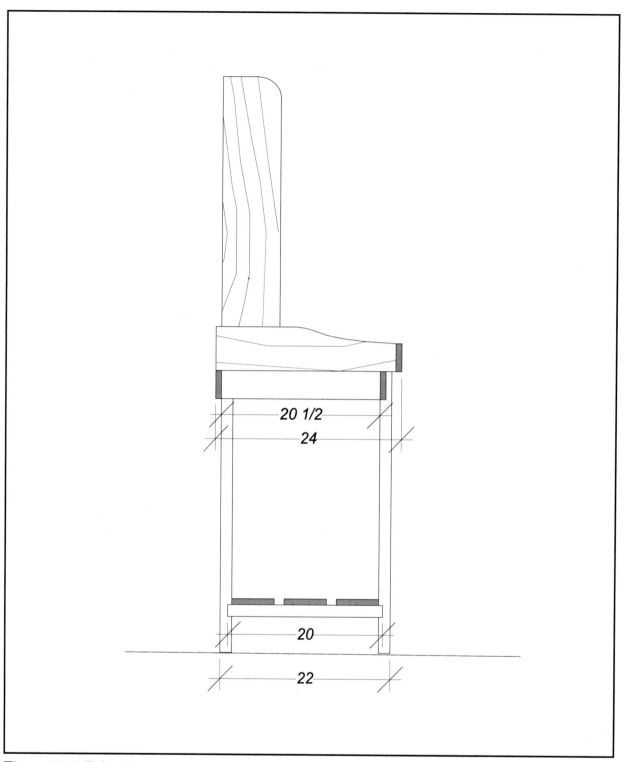

Figure 14.2. Side view

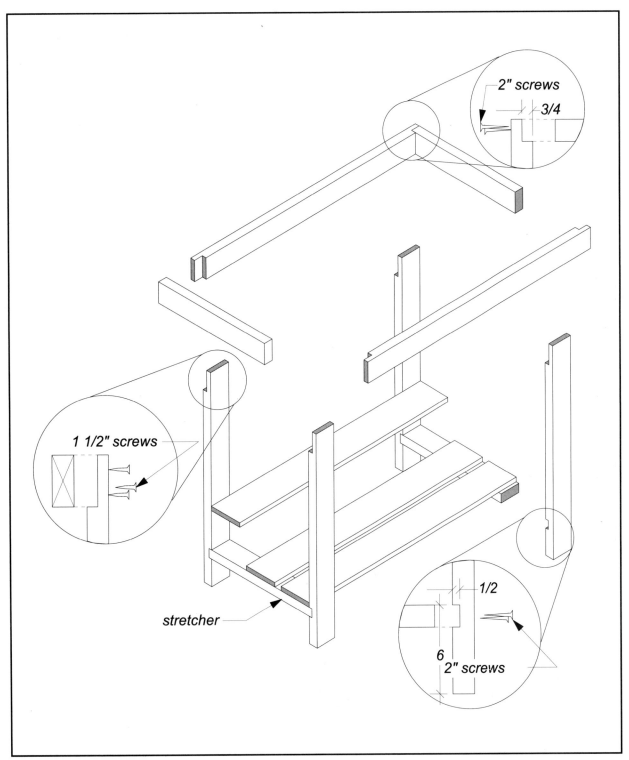

Figure 14.3. Exploded view of table frame

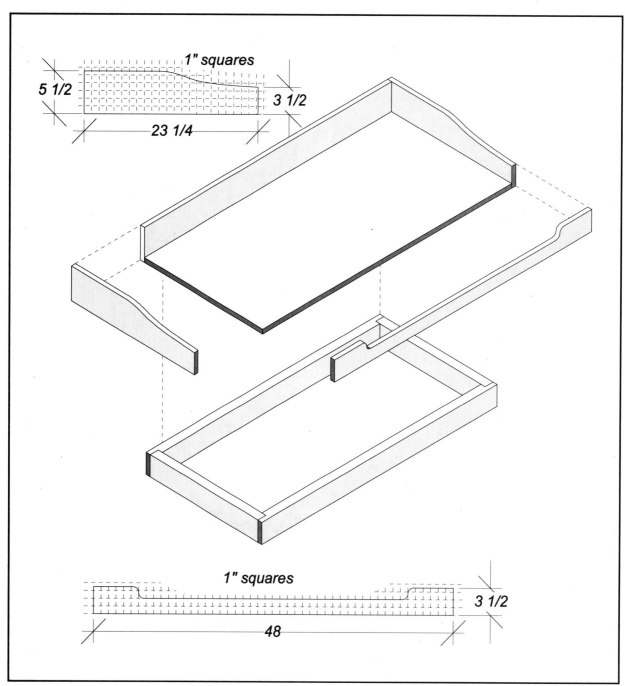

1" squares

5 1/2

3 1/2

23 1/4

1" squares

3 1/2

48

Figure 14.4. Exploded view of table, with patterns

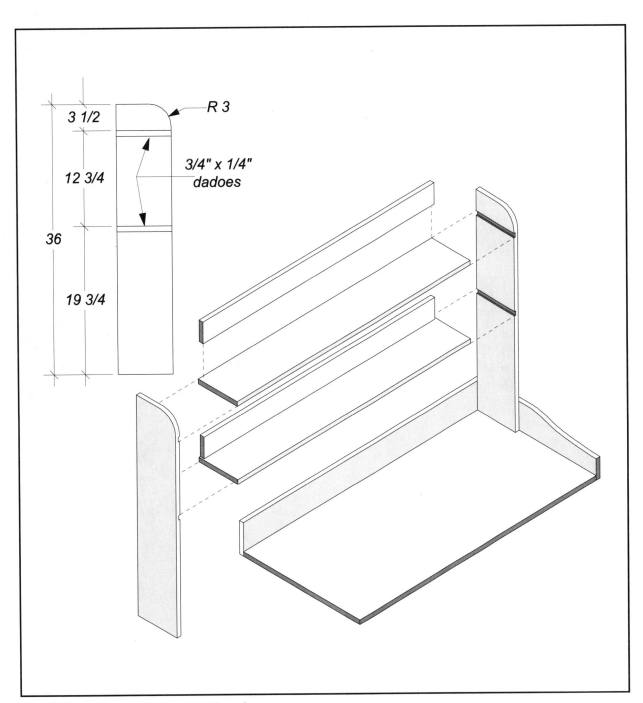

Figure 14.5. Exploded view of hutch

· Project 15 ·
GREENHOUSE

A greenhouse isn't absolutely necessary for a successful garden, but it does add an exciting dimension to gardening. Spring comes early to a greenhouse, which makes it the ideal place for starting vegetables. And a greenhouse is also a great place to perk up those houseplants that suffer from the winter blahs.

You can build this greenhouse for less than half the price of a kit of similar materials and dimensions. It's framed with 2×2s and 2×4s on a foundation of 2×6s. Heat-sensitive mechanisms automatically open and close the vents. The sheathing material is a double-wall extruded polycarbonate sheet with an ultraviolet protective coating on the outside surface. The ribs that form the double walls must run vertically. The illustrated project is made from 4×8-foot sheets 5/16 inches (8 millimeters) thick, but you can also use 1/4-inch (6-millimeter)

sheets. The bottom edges of the sheathing are sealed with a perforated vent tape of either aluminum or fabric. The sheathing described here is manufactured by Polygal USA, Inc., 2352 Highway 14 West, Janesville, WI 53545.

To find local suppliers of greenhouse materials, check the Yellow Pages of your telephone book. Look under "Greenhouse Equipment and Supplies" and "Lawn and Garden Equipment and Supplies."

MAKING THE FOUNDATION

Cut the pieces for the foundation according to the dimensions shown in Figure 15.2. You can use 2×6s throughout or use 2×4s for the interior partitions. The partitions form a center aisle, which can be paved with brick, and four beds in which you can start plants directly.

When cutting the pieces, take care to

Project 15 Materials List

Description	Quantity	Length in feet	Comments
2×6	7	8	Foundation
2×4	14	8	Main ribs, rails, benches, shelf
2×2	17	8	Trusses, collar ties, misc.
2×2	20	12	Ribs, studs, braces, misc.
1×4		100	Benches, shelves
Angle brackets	38		
Trim		200	1/2" bender board stock
5/16" sheathing	9		Sheets, 4×8, polycarbonate
3" screws			As needed
1½" screws			As needed
2½" screws			As needed
1" screws			Low-profile, as needed
1" screws			With neoprene washers, as needed
Vent openers	3		Optional
Hardware, misc.			As needed, see text

make the ends square. Use 3-inch screws or 16d galvanized nails to hold the foundation together. Build the foundation on a flat surface. Check that the foundation is square by measuring the diagonals (when each diagonal measurement is the same, the foundation is square). Nail a long 1×4 diagonally across the frame to hold it square as you move it into place.

If wind is not a problem in your area, you can level the foundation on cement blocks. I used 2×4 stakes 16 inches long driven into the ground at the inside corners and in the middle of each wall. Then I nailed the foundation to the stakes. This holds the foundation level and adequately anchors it in place.

MAKING AND RAISING THE SIDE WALLS

The side walls rise at an 85-degree angle. To make the side walls, cut the six main ribs out of 2×4s 72¼ inches long with parallel 5-degree angles at each end as shown in Figure 15.3. Then notch the ends as shown in the inset. Take care to keep the top and bottom ends correctly oriented.

Cut the top and bottoms rails, or plates, 96 inches long, and rip a 5-degree bevel along one edge.

Begin the side wall assembly by placing two of the main ribs notch side (outside) up on a flat surface (see Figure 15.4). Place the top and bottom rails in the notches, making sure the beveled edges are correctly oriented (the bevels should be facing outward and flush with the ends of the ribs). Also make sure the ends of the rails are flush with the outer surfaces of the ribs. Fasten the rails to the ribs with two 2½-inch screws at each end.

Locate the center of each rail, and fasten the middle rib into place. Now locate the center of each of the areas formed by the main ribs. Measure the distance between the rails, and cut the secondary ribs to fit (the ends

will be square). Use an angle bracket at each end, with 1-inch low-profile, wafer-head screws (see Figure 15.13).

Locate the horizontal center of the wall, and add the 2×2 blocks between each rib, again using two 2½-inch screws at each end.

Square up the wall assembly and temporarily brace it. Take a piece of 2×2 stock and, holding it in place where shown in Figures 15.4 and 15.5, scribe the angles to fit. Secure the braces with two 2½-inch screws at each end.

Refer to Figures 15.5 and 15.6 for details on raising the side walls.

First, temporarily tack the bottom rail to the greenhouse foundation. Then fasten the wall securely to the foundation with a 1¼×9-inch steel strap with low-profile screws, as shown in the lower inset in Figure 15.5, at each main rib.

Next, cut a pair of collar ties 74¼ inches long and with opposing 5-degree bevels at each end as shown in Figure 15.6. Screw the collar ties in place as shown in the upper inset in Figure 15.5.

Make a mark on the foundation 10 inches in from each side. Use a level with a straightedge to check the walls. The walls are at the correct inclination when the upper inside point of each wall is plumb with its corresponding mark, as shown in Figure 15.6. (*Important:* This will be true only so long as all actual measurements conform exactly to the drawings. If not, make the inclination the same on both sides.) Temporarily brace the walls in place.

FRAMING IN THE END WALLS

To frame in the back wall, cut three 2×2 studs 72 inches long. Lay out the studs as shown in Figure 15.7. Use angle brackets to secure the studs to the foundation, and drive a single 2½-inch screw through each stud and into the collar tie at the top.

When you add the horizontal blocking, be careful not to push the studs one way or the other by forcing the angled pieces (those that abut the side walls) into place.

Now add the braces. To get the correct length of each brace, hold a piece of 2×2 in the opening against the studs and mark the angles at each end. Secure the braces with 2½-inch screws.

Frame the front wall, as shown in Figure 15.8, in the same manner as the back.

MAKING AND INSTALLING THE ROOF TRUSSES

Each of the five roof trusses is composed of a bottom chord, two top chords, and two struts. Each end truss has an additional header to form the exhaust vent openings. All the truss components are made of 2×2s.

Cut the bottom chords 77 inches long, with opposing 60-degree angles on each end.

The top chords are 41½ inches long and have a 30-degree angle at the top and a 60-degree angle at the bottom. Following the assembly procedure shown in Figure 15.9, begin by fastening the top chords to the bottom chord with two 1½-inch screws. Then fasten the top chords at the peak with two 1½-inch screws.

The struts are 12⅛ inches long with a 30-degree angle at the upper end. The headers are 24 inches long.

Lay out the trusses on the top rails of the side walls. The end trusses are flush with the end walls, the middle truss is centered between the ends, and the remaining trusses are centered between the center and end trusses.

Tack the trusses in place by driving a screw or nail through the angle cut in the ends of the bottom chords. Sight down the peak to ensure that the trusses are in alignment. Permanently anchor the trusses with angles as shown in the inset of Figure 15.10 and in Figure 15.13. Next, install blocking as shown in Figure 15.10. Use two 2½-inch screws at each joint, driven at the necessary angle. Measure the blocks as you go, mak-

ing sure you don't force the gables out of plumb.

SHEATHING THE GREENHOUSE

The greenhouse can be sheathed with a minimum of nine 4×8 polycarbonate sheets. Figure 15.11 shows the cutting pattern for each sheet. Use a scratch awl or a sharp pencil with soft lead to mark the panels. Note that one surface has a coating to protect against the effects of ultraviolet rays; this coating *must* be facing out. Each sheet comes with a protective film on both sides. When possible, keep this film in place while cutting to avoid scratching the material.

Cut the sheathing with a circular saw mounted with a fine-tooth blade. The cutting action creates a static charge, and much of the dust will be taken into the cells between the walls of the material. Use a vacuum cleaner to extract the dust after each cut.

Cover the exposed lower edges of each sheet with ventilating tape. This allows for airflow between the layers but prevents bugs from crawling inside.

The primary fastening mechanism for the sheathing is the battens, which are held in place by either low-profile or trumpet-head screws. In some instances, however, you will need to fasten the sheathing in an area where there is no batten. For this purpose, use screws with self-sealing neoprene washers as shown in Figure 15.14.

Cut and install the roof sheathing first. The roof sheathing hangs over the side walls about 3½ inches but is flush with the end walls. Tack the pieces in place until they are correctly aligned. Then use two neoprene screws in the center of each panel, one in the crosspiece between the trusses, and one along the top rail of the side wall.

Next, cut and install the sheathing on the side walls. At 73 inches long, the material overhangs the foundation by about 1 inch. The side-wall sheathing tucks right underneath the roof sheathing. Be careful not to force the roof sheathing up higher than it should be. Use neoprene screws to hold the panels in place.

Cut the center panel for the rear wall next. For greatest accuracy, hold a full sheet in place against the wall and mark where to cut. The panel also should hang 1 inch below the foundation. Cut out the intake and exhaust vents before installing the panel.

Similarly, mark and cut the left and right rear panels. Notice in Figure 15.11 that the remaining portions of each piece rotate to form the opposite-side panels for the front wall. Don't flip the panels—this would put the ultraviolet coating on the inside.

Complete the front wall, leaving the door and vent areas open.

ADDING THE BATTENS AND TRIM

All the trim on the greenhouse is cut from ½-inch bender board stock ripped 1⅝ inches wide. (Cedar bender board comes in thicknesses of ¼ and ½ inch and is 3½ inches wide. It is used as a lawn edging and can bend to some degree to go around curves.) You can, however, use ¾-inch stock if you choose.

If you wish to paint or stain the trim, apply the first coat before installation.

This greenhouse is not entirely watertight. Especially during a heavy rain, water will seep under the battens and between the panel seams. To eliminate much of this seepage, use a good-quality latex or silicone caulking between the seams and under the panel edges before applying the battens and trim.

To apply the trim, begin with the ridge cap, which is made of two pieces left full width. Rip a 30-degree bevel on one edge of each piece, and nail them together, as shown in Figure 15.15, with 3d or 4d galvanized nails. Make the ridge cap at least 98 inches long, so that it will extend beyond the sheathing and trim you eventually will apply to the front and back walls. Screw the ridge cap in place.

Next, do the side walls, covering the seam between the two panels, and keeping the corner pieces flush with the front and back wall surfaces.

Now add the gable pieces, cutting the lower ends flush with the corner pieces on the side walls.

Add the corner pieces on the front and back walls flush with pieces on the side walls (see Figure 15.16).

The battens on the roof come next. Place the outer pieces flush with the surface of the gable trim.

Finally, trim the door and vent openings.

MAKING AND INSTALLING THE FRONT AND VENT DOORS

The front and vent doors are framed from 2×2s, the corners held together with angles. You can make a one-piece front door or split it in half as a Dutch door. Notice in Figure 15.11 that the sheathing for the door comes from what's left over after cutting two side-wall panels. When building the front door, frame in a length of 2×2 stock wherever there is a seam between panel pieces. If you want a door without any seams, you will have to purchase a tenth sheet of sheathing material.

Make the doors about ⅜ inch smaller than their openings. Before tacking on the sheathing, make sure each door is square. Trim the doors in the same manner as the rest of the greenhouse.

Use good-quality hinges for the doors. Make sure they swing freely. Automatic vent openers (Figure 15.17) are optional. Install according to the manufacturer's instructions.

Add latches and other door hardware of your choice.

MAKING THE BENCHES AND SHELVES

Although the logical sequence of construction indicates that the benches and shelves be installed last, consider installing them before sheathing the greenhouse. On a hot, sunny day, the temperature inside will get well above 100 degrees.

The benches, shown in Figure 15.18, are split in the middle, hinged to the wall, and supported with a length of chain at each end. Hinging the benches is a handy option that adds versatility to your greenhouse. It makes cleanup easier, makes it easier to work in the raised beds beneath, and allows for growth of tall plants like tomatoes. The benches are held in the up position with hook-and-eye fasteners, or gate hooks.

To make the hinged benches, first mount a 2×4 along the length of the side wall with 2½-inch screws. Put it at a comfortable height for the person who will eventually use the greenhouse, anywhere from 30 to 36 inches from the finished floor.

Make the frame 20 inches deep by half the distance between the inside walls, less about ½ inch.

Make the surface of the benches out of 1×4s 21 inches long. Space them about 1 inch or so apart, and keep them flush with the back edge of the frame. Use a pair of 3½-inch T hinges for each bench. Support the benches with chain, S hooks, and screw eyes. To make the benches level, adjust the length of the chain and the position of the screw eyes.

The upper shelf is similar to the bench. It is made of two lengths of 2×4, surfaced with 1×4s cut 8 inches long.

Screw the shelves to the main ribs, and support them at the front with chain hung from the trusses.

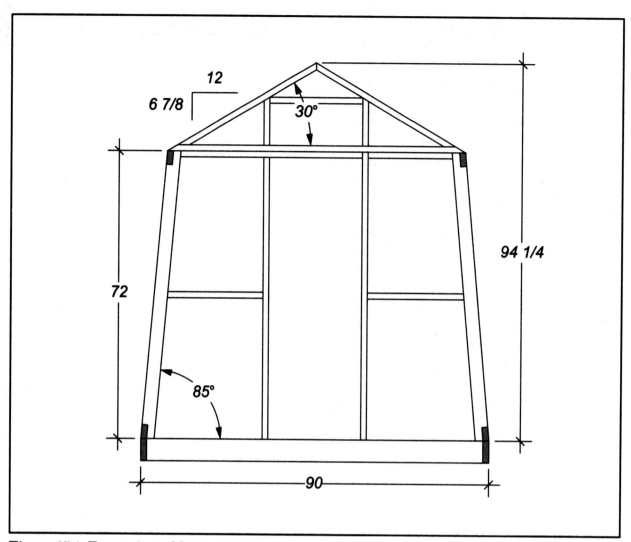

Figure 15.1. Front view of frame

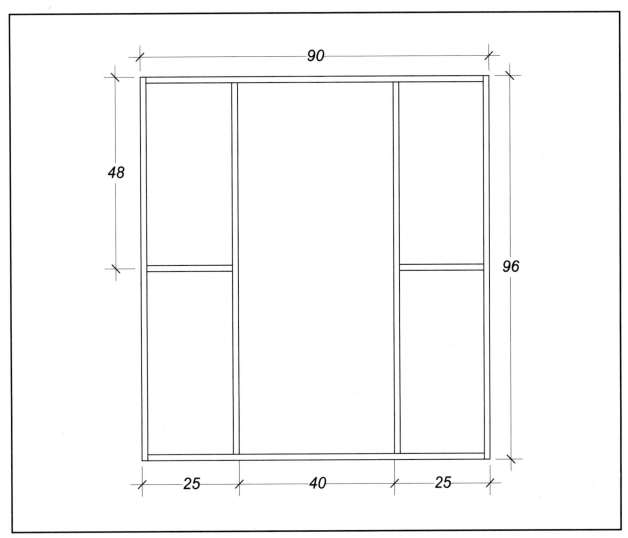

Figure 15.2. Foundation plan

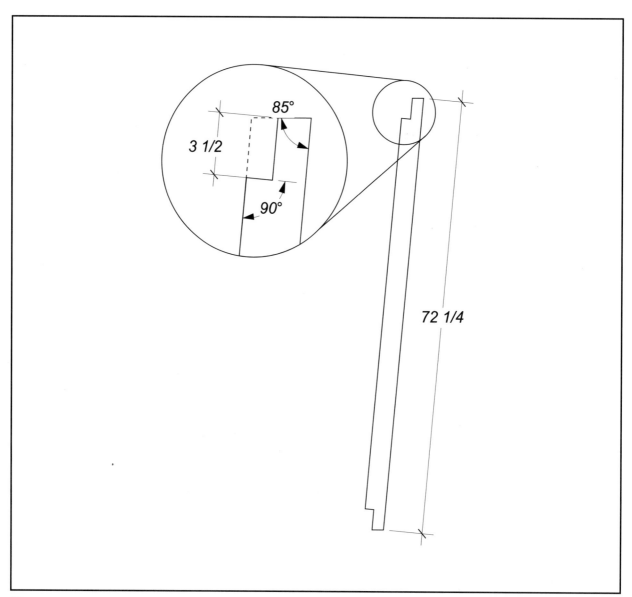

Figure 15.3. Main rib detail

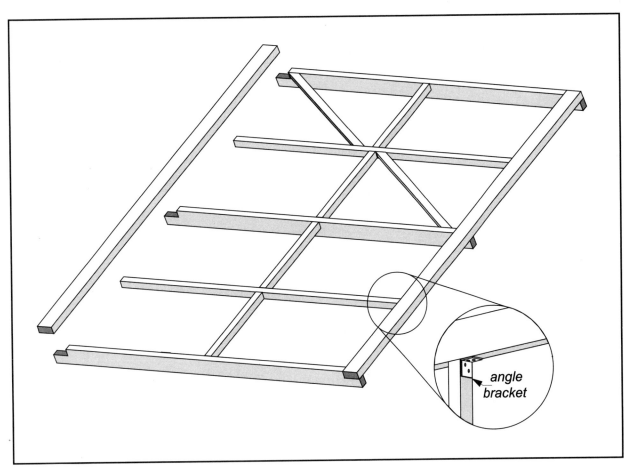

Figure 15.4. Side wall assembly detail

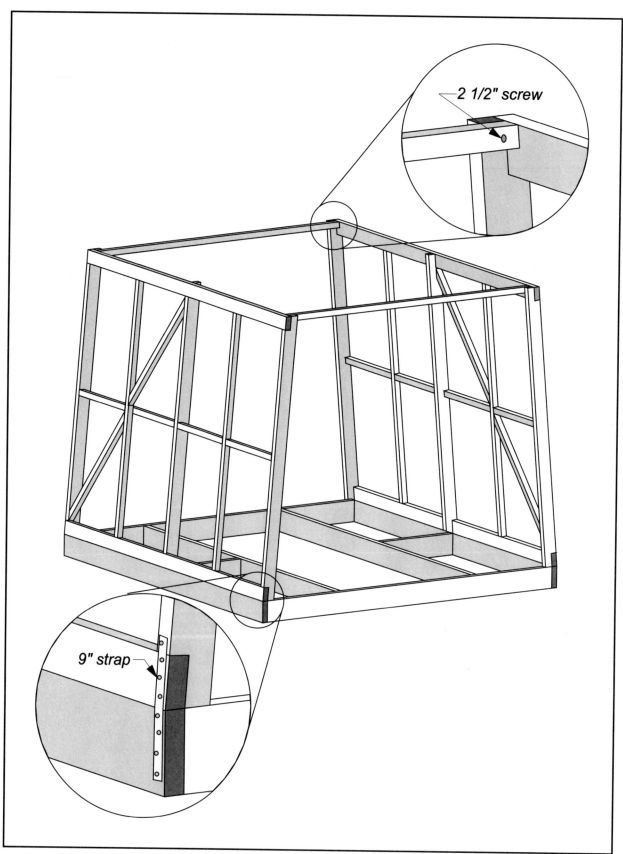

2 1/2" screw

9" strap

Figure 15.5. Raising the side walls

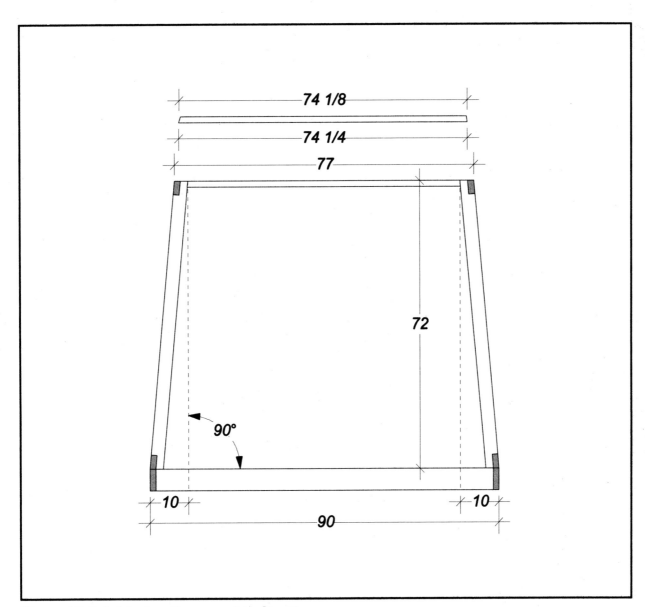

Figure 15.6. Achieving the correct inclination

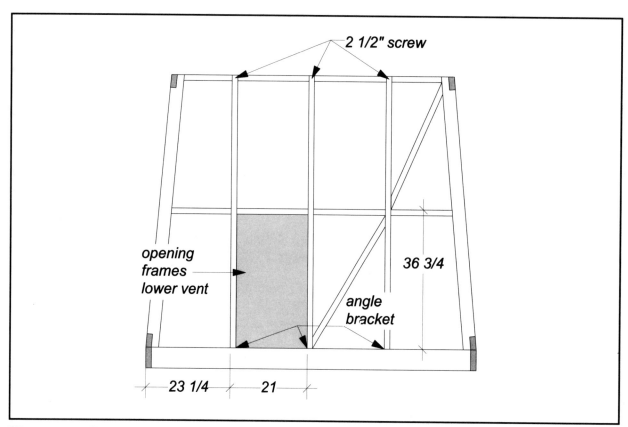

Figure 15.7. Framing the rear wall, as seen from the outside

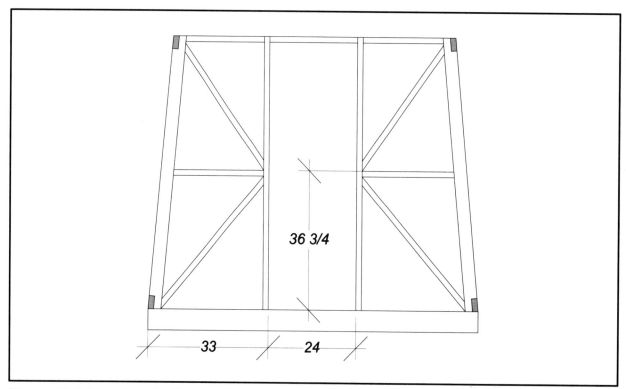

Figure 15.8. Framing the front wall

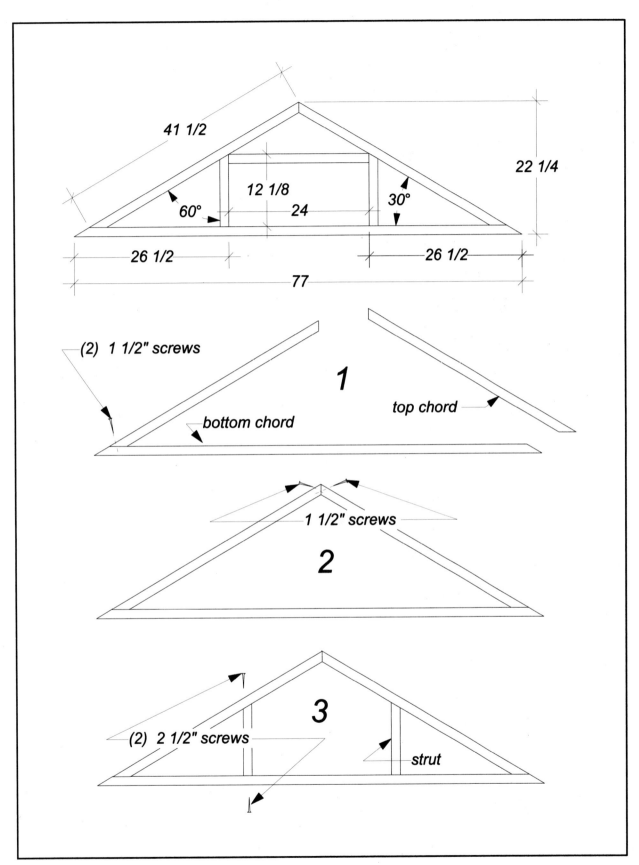

Figure 15.9. Building the trusses

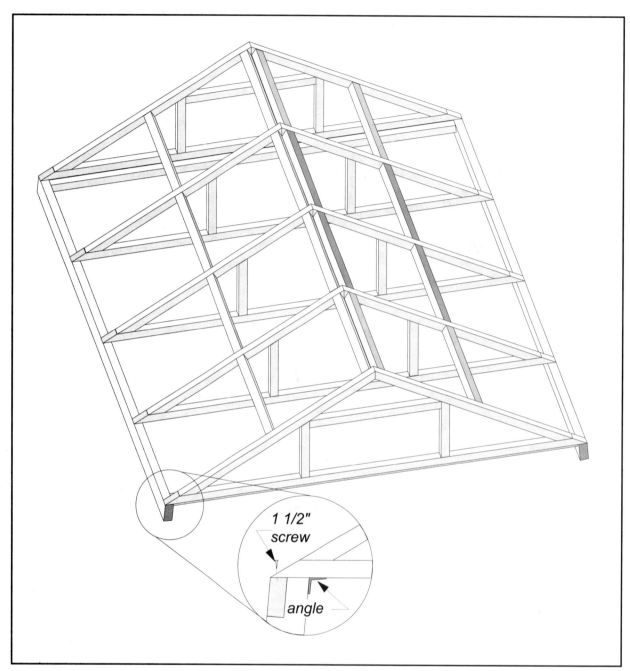

Figure 15.10. Roof assembly

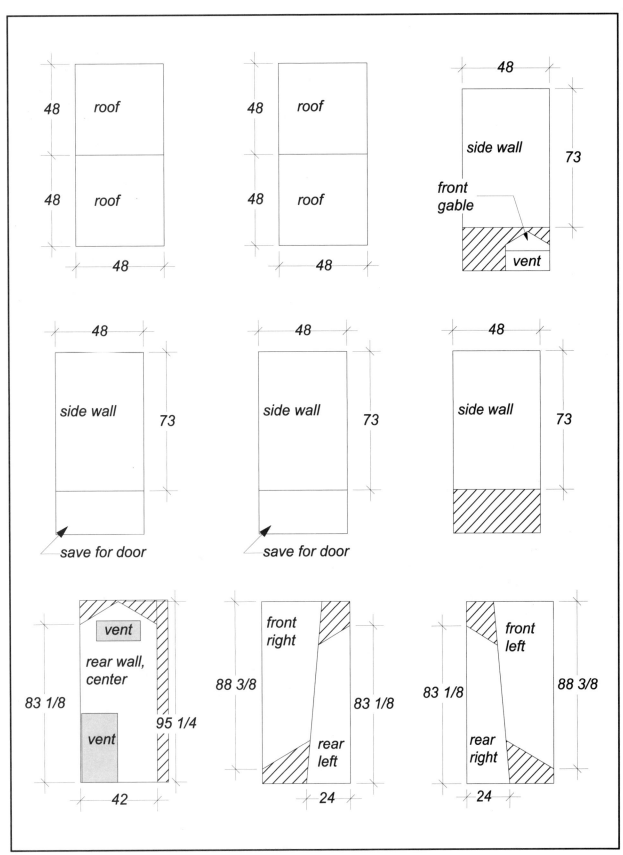

Figure 15.11. Sheathing cutting scheme

Figure 15.12. Some of the materials used are ⁵⁄₁₆-inch polycarbonate sheathing, 1½- and 2½-inch exterior trumpet-head screws, 1-inch wafer-head screws, 1-inch neoprene screws, interior angles, and 9-inch strap ties.

Figure 15.13. Angles hold intermediate ribs and trusses in place

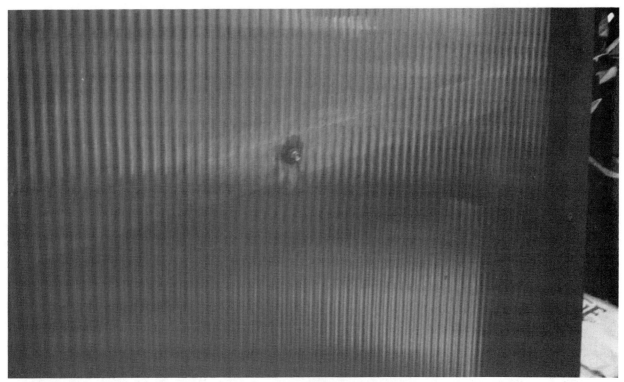

Figure 15.14. Use screws with neoprene washers to hold sheathing where no battens occur.

Figure 15.15. Bevel the upper edge of each of the ridge pieces and tack them together. Let the ridge overhang at the ends.

Figure 15.16. Trim detail at gable overhang

Figure 15.17. Automatic vent openers control ventilation.

Figure 15.18. Benches are hinged and hung on chain so that they can be raised out of the way.

▪ Metric Conversions ▪

INCHES TO MILLIMETRES

MM	IN.	MM
25.4	51	1295.4
50.8	52	1320.8
76.2	53	1346.2
101.6	54	1371.6
127.0	55	1397.0
152.4	56	1422.4
177.8	57	1447.8
203.2	58	1473.2
228.6	59	1498.6
254.0	60	1524.0
279.4	61	1549.4
304.8	62	1574.8
330.2	63	1600.2
355.6	64	1625.6
381.0	65	1651.0
406.4	66	1676.4
431.8	67	1701.8
457.2	68	1727.2
482.6	69	1752.6
508.0	70	1778.0
533.4	71	1803.4
558.8	72	1828.8
584.2	73	1854.2
609.6	74	1879.6
635.0	75	1905.0
660.4	76	1930.4
685.8	77	1955.8
711.2	78	1981.2
736.6	79	2006.6
762.0	80	2032.0
787.4	81	2057.4
812.8	82	2082.8
838.2	83	2108.2
863.6	84	2133.6
889.0	85	2159.0
914.4	86	2184.4
939.8	87	2209.8
965.2	88	2235.2
990.6	89	2260.6
1016.0	90	2286.0
1041.4	91	2311.4
1066.8	92	2336.8
1092.2	93	2362.2
1117.6	94	2387.6
1143.0	95	2413.0
1168.4	96	2438.4
1193.8	97	2463.8
1219.2	98	2489.2
1244.6	99	2514.6
1270.0	100	2540.0

bove table is exact on the basis: 1 in. = 25.4 mm

U.S. TO METRIC

1 inch = 2.540 centimetres
1 foot = .305 metre
1 yard = .914 metre
1 mile = 1.609 kilometres

METRIC TO U.S.

1 millimetre = .039 inch
1 centimetre = .394 inch
1 metre = 3.281 feet or 1.094 yards
1 kilometre = .621 mile

INCH-METRIC EQUIVALENTS

FRACTION	DECIMAL EQUIVALENT CUSTOMARY (IN.)	METRIC (MM)	FRACTION	DECIMAL EQUIVALENT CUSTOMARY (IN.)	METRIC (MM)
	1/64———.015	0.3969		33/64———.515	13.0969
1/32———.031		0.7938	17/32———.531		13.4938
	3/64———.046	1.1906		35/64———.546	13.8906
1/16———.062		1.5875	9/16———.562		14.2875
	5/64———.078	1.9844		37/64———.578	14.6844
3/32———.093		2.3813	19/32———.593		15.0813
	7/64———.109	2.7781		39/64———.609	15.4781
1/8———.125		3.1750	5/8———.625		15.8750
	9/64———.140	3.5719		41/64———.640	16.2719
5/32———.156		3.9688	21/32———.656		16.6688
	11/64———.171	4.3656		43/64———.671	17.0656
3/16———.187		4.7625	11/16———.687		17.4625
	13/64———.203	5.1594		45/64———.703	17.8594
7/32———.218		5.5563	23/32———.718		18.2563
	15/64———.234	5.9531		47/64———.734	18.6531
1/4———.250		6.3500	3/4———.750		19.0500
	17/64———.265	6.7469		49/64———.765	19.4469
9/32———.281		7.1438	25/32———.781		19.8438
	19/64———.296	7.5406		51/64———.796	20.2406
5/16———.312		7.9375	13/16———.812		20.6375
	21/64———.328	8.3384		53/64———.828	21.0344
11/32———.343		8.7313	27/32———.843		21.4313
	23/64———.359	9.1281		55/64———.859	21.8281
3/8———.375		9.5250	7/8———.875		22.2250
	25/64———.390	9.9219		57/64———.890	22.6219
13/32———.406		10.3188	29/32———.906		23.0188
	27/64———.421	10.7156		59/64———.921	23.4156
7/16———.437		11.1125	15/16———.937		23.8125
	29/64———.453	11.5094		61/64———.953	24.2094
15/32———.468		11.9063	31/32———.968		24.6063
	31/64———.484	12.3031		63/64———.984	25.0031
1/2———.500		12.7000	1———1.000		25.4000